The Reluctant Vision

The Reluctant Vision

*An Essay in
the Philosophy
of Religion*

T. PATRICK BURKE

FORTRESS PRESS   Philadelphia

Portions of an earlier draft of this book, especially of what is now Chapters 1 and 2, were published in an essay, "Theology as Part of the Study of the Phenomenon of Religion," in Maurice Friedman, T. Patrick Burke, and Samuel Laeuchli, *Searching in the Syntax of Things* (Philadelphia: Fortress Press, 1972).

Copyright © 1974 by Fortress Press

Library of Congress Catalog Card Number 73-88354

ISBN 0-8006-1068-7

4025H73   Printed in U.S.A.   1-1068

Table of Contents

Introduction

> Hui Tzu said to Chuang Tzu, "Your words are useless!" Chuang Tzu said, "A man has to understand the useless before you can talk to him about the useful. The earth is certainly vast and broad, though a man uses no more of it than the area he puts his feet on. If, however, you were to dig away all the earth from around his feet until you reached the Yellow Springs, then would the man still be able to make use of it?" "No, it would be useless," said Hui Tzu. "It is obvious, then," said Chuang Tzu, "that the useless has its use."
>
> — Chuang Tzu

Most people will grant that potatoes are important. Discourse about potatoes, however, does not enjoy the same popularity as potatoes. When the chips are down, talk about potatoes is just no substitute for the original thing. Your speaker about potatoes cannot count on getting the same uninhibited welcome accorded as a matter of course to the french fry or well-baked Idaho. So it is with religion. Few will deny that religion is important. But discourse about the phenomenon of religion cannot claim a comparably widespread interest. In comparison with religion, talk about religion is remote and uninspiring. Yet talk about religion has its own importance. Our religion changes as our ideas about it change. That our ideas about it will change is certain. They will change as the ideas current in society change, which is happening all the time. They will change, as our ideas about so many other things do, just by the fact that we get older. There is a question whether we

1

will let these changes take place in us unconsciously and haphazardly, according to the prevailing winds, or whether we will take the reins of our thought in our own hands, and guide our own inner development.

The prevailing current in philosophy of religion is seriously deficient on at least two counts. First, it is not a philosophy of the phenomenon of religion, but of one particular religion, Christianity, and not even of Christianity as such, but of one part of it, namely, metaphysical conceptions associated with it. Of Chinese religions it has nothing to say, nor of those of Indian origin, nor even of Islam, so close to the Judeo-Christian tradition. Its horizons are blinkered by a theological tradition. Even Judaism is not treated as a religion, but only insofar as some of its ideas have contributed to Christian thought. It is doubtful whether this narrow sight was ever justified, given the wide reach of intellectual commerce in even the remote past. Today it is not only inexcusable, it is uninteresting.

If even Christianity were treated with some degree of wholeness, as a phenomenon in its own right, a special sort of community existing in history, rather than a metaphysical system only, more insight might be gained. We would not have philosophy of religion, but at least we would have a philosophy of Christianity. But Christianity is treated as if it existed outside of history and without community. Attention is concentrated on two metaphysical questions, the existence of God and the immortality of the soul, and these owe as much to Plato as to the New Testament!

If even these two ideas were treated with the breadth and comprehensiveness we have a right to expect of philosophy, we might be more satisfied. But they are dealt with from the impoverished standpoint of one particular perspective, the language used about them. Not that the focus on language has been unfruitful; on the contrary, it has been enlightening, and no doubt will continue to be. But the phenomenon of religion is not exhausted by its language. The language philosophy that many philosophers of religion take as their base is still permeated by a naive and uncritical positivism, unaware of its own social and historical relativity. It happens not infrequently that what a person says in one place he forgets in another, so that even philosophers otherwise aware of the social relativity of knowledge fail to take it into account when they deal with language and the language of religion. Language is an excellent place to start in investigating the phenomenon of religion. It is a desperate place to finish.

The method employed in this essay could perhaps be called functional analysis. That is, it is an attempt to analyze the structure of the phenomenon of religion as revealed by the way it functions. As applied here, the method has three main features. First, it is not associated with any particular existing philosophical school. It makes no assumptions of either an empiricist or an existentialist nature, for example. It simply interrogates the phenomenon as to how it functions. It would like to let the phenomenon speak for itself; but alas the phenomenon refuses to speak for itself. It is inevitable that the one who undertakes to speak on its behalf will impose his own presuppositions onto it. But the method does not aim at imposing presuppositions. It would prefer to remove them, so far as possible. The usual manner of doing philosophy of religion has been to commence with some already existing philosophy, be it empiricism, idealism, pragmatism or what have you, and then to apply it in the field of religion. The method offered here stands in contrast to that.

The task of philosophy itself is conceived of quite broadly in this essay. Philosophy is distinguished from other enterprises by the generality of its interest and its conceptions. A philosophical insight has a higher degree of abstraction and a broader range. It is a common notion that abstract ideas are useless. Nothing could be further from the truth. It is precisely the more abstract idea which is the more useful, because it applies to a greater number and variety of particular cases. By the same token of course more abstract ideas are also more dangerous if they are misguided. The task of philosophy as envisaged here is to arrive at those insights which are most general and therefore most abstract.

The second feature of the method used here is its emphasis on the disclosure of structures and functions rather than of "essence" on the one hand or of truth and falsity on the other. It is not an attempt either to justify or to arraign either the phenomenon of religion in general, or any particular religion. The truth question cannot be excluded from the study of religion, but up to the present time no generally acceptable method of handling it has been developed, and it is treated here as subservient to the question of function. Perhaps an approach to the question of truth by means of the question of function may prove more fruitful.

Similarly, functional analysis is not an attempt to lay bare the "essence" of the phenomenon of religion, or of any particular religion. The phenomenon of religion is a bundle of diverse historical activities that we have tied together into a package and put a common label on. An investigation of the phenomenon of religion is an enquiry whether these diverse activities exhibit any commonality of function and structure. The fact that English and other languages, though not all, now work with a unifying term "religion" for these activities provides prima facie grounds for undertaking such an enquiry. If a commonality of function should emerge, it may serve as well as an essence.

The task of philosophy of religion then is to arrive at

insights into the function and functional structure of religions which will have a greater breadth, a larger generality, a greater abstraction than the more particular insights of other disciplines.

The notion of function is developed further in chapter 3. For a beginning it may be taken quite simply as the way the thing works. It is not to be confused with the narrow approach sometimes known as "functionalism" which sees in things nothing more than certain specific kinds of function, such as the sociological, the psychological, etc. As applied to religion it deals with the characteristically religious function of religious ideas and communities. It takes the notion of "religious" on its own terms, and does not attempt to reduce it to any factor or group of factors that are not religious, unless such a reduction should be demonstrated to be necessary. To decide what constitutes the characteristically religious function of a religious statement is one of the first occupations of the essay.

The third feature of the method employed here is that its scope is not restricted to one particular religion, Christianity, let alone to the metaphysical ideas historically associated with Christianity. It is an analysis of the phenomenon of religion in general. It accords equal weight to the religions of Chinese and Indian as to those of Semitic origin. For practical reasons it concentrates on the major religions, because these have written documents in which their various points of view have been elaborated publicly and are more accessible.

The presentation is expository rather than argumentative, that is, the argument lies in the exhibition of perspectives. This way of proceeding is rather like filling in a canvas. The initial moves are partial; one begins by pencilling a line in here and another one there, and the composition of the whole emerges only gradually. It does not present itself entirely at the beginning, but cumulates to the end. It asks to be judged at the end, rather than by the probationary and partial statements made at the beginning.

This essay is an attempt to weave into a more or less cohering synthesis strands dispersed in many places. Its aim is to exhibit one man's perspective. I have been concerned to present a picture, rather than to justify it. The essay is an invitation to "look at it this way." A painting does not provide independent grounds to justify itself: it offers itself to the viewer, commending itself by the way it fits together. This is not to object to argument, or declare grounds unnecessary. But it is a truism that argument is usually in the service of a prior point of view, and those who feel deeply enough about a position can usually discover arguments sufficient to make it appear at least reasonable. It seemed better in this instance just to present the point of view, and let it be accepted or rejected on its own merits, as it were. It is a piece of autobiography, marking a long voyage in the author's thoughts and emotions.

Practically every sentence here either is indebted to some other writer, or can be found elsewhere, though the creditors are rarely named in the text or quoted. In his preface to the *Phenomenology of Mind*, Hegel remarks, "By determining the relation which a philosophical work professes to have to other treatises on the same subject, an extraneous interest is introduced, and obscurity is thrown over the point at issue." I agree with this in principle. However, notes are provided for each chapter which perhaps may serve, if not to satisfy the desire for support of positions taken, at least to provide background for them.

The reader should be put on guard that the style is sometimes compressed. It may appear that something is being said by the fact that its opposite is not being said. I can only commend the essay's obvious flaws to the charity which any reader may be presumed to have who goes to the lengths of picking it up.

NOTE

1. The deplorable constriction of interest that philosophy of religion has fallen into can be seen from even a brief perusal of the scope or range of some prominent current works. Two texts widely used at the present time are John Hick's *Philosophy of Religion* (N.J., Prentice-Hall, 1963) and Frederick Ferré's *Basic Modern Philosophy of Religion* (New York: Scribner's, 1967). Both illustrate well the contemporary situation in the discipline. Ferré gives a definition of religion that is far broader than traditional western theism, namely, "a way of valuing most comprehensively and intensively." He explicitly considers this definition extensive enough to include classical Buddhism and Jainism. Yet he restricts his entire subsequent treatment to "the actual religious tradition dominant in our Western heritage," i.e., theism. The discipline is then exhausted in this view in the questions of proofs for the existence of the theistic God, and of language about that God. The theistic language studied is restricted for the most part to Protestant Christian language.

Hick's work similarly is confined to proofs and disproofs for the existence of the Judeo-Christian God, the immortality of the soul, and "religious language" which again does not go beyond language about the Judeo-Christian God. In neither case do the authors philosophize about the phenomenon of religion itself.

A similar restriction of "religion" to "Western theism" and of "philosophy" to the particular standpoint of contemporary philosophy characterizes: Peter A. Bertocci, *Introduction to the Philosophy of Religion* (New York: Prentice-Hall, 1951), Geddes MacGregor, *Introduction to Religious Philosophy* (Boston: Houghton-Mifflin, 1959), Thomas McPherson, *The Philosophy of Religion* (London: Van Nostrand, 1965), and J. L. Goodall, *An Introduction to the Philosophy of Religion* (London: Longmans, 1966—this book is even more narrowly confined to Christian perspectives than most). H. D. Lewis, *Philosophy of Religion* (London: E.U.P., 1965) goes somewhat beyond western theism in a short chapter on mysticism, and a very brief one on "other religions" as a sort of appendix.

The same relentlessly Western, even Anglo-Saxon tunnel vision is a feature of the following collections of readings: Daniel Bronstein and Harold Schulweis, *Approaches to the Philosophy of Religion* (Englewood Cliffs, N.J.: Prentice-Hall, 1954) which gives much attention to the exclusively Christian problem of church and state; Geddes MacGregor and J. Wesley Robb, *Readings in Religious Philosophy* (Boston: Houghton-Mifflin, 1962); John Hick, *Classical and Contemporary Readings in the Philosophy of Religion* (Englewood Cliffs: Prentice-Hall, 1964); George L. Abernethy and Thomas A. Langford, *Philosophy of Religion* (London: Macmillan, 1968); and Basil Mitchell, *The Philosophy of Religion* (Oxford, 1971), which simply equates religion with the religion of Englishmen, and philosophy with the philosophy of Englishmen, with no hint that things worthy of interest might be found elsewhere. John A. Mourant's *Readings in the Philosophy of Religion* (New York: Crowell, 1954) provides a little relief, giving a few pages from Shankara, Patanjali, and the Lankavatara Scripture. It should be remarked, of course, that this restriction of interest does not prevent some of the works named from making valuable contributions within their scope; this is especially true of McPherson's.

A few contemporary works represent an improvement on those listed above in that although their conception of "religion" goes scarcely or not at all beyond Western theism, their notion of philosophy does extend farther than contemporary Western analysis. The better examples of these tend to be histories, however, rather than philosophies. James Collins' *The Emergence of Philosophy of Religion* (Yale, 1967) is a study of Hume, Kant and Hegel in relation to theism. M. J. Charlesworth, *Philosophy of Religion: The Historic Approaches*, (London: Macmillan, 1972) surveys the relationship of philosophy and religion over the past two thousand years of Western thought. Charlesworth admits that his view of religion is myopic, but attempts to justify it nonetheless. E. S. Brightman, *A Philosophy of Religion* (Prentice-Hall, 1940) concentrates on the ideas of God and immortality, but includes a valuable chapter on the problem of human purpose. E. A. Burtt, *Types of Religious Philosophy* (New York: Harper, 1939, revised ed., 1951) is an enterprise not unlike Charlesworth's more recent one, an attempt "to describe

the most influential positions in Western religious philosophy."
In light of the same author's excellent collection of Buddhist
documents, and of his perceptive analysis of the relationship of
Eastern and Western philosophy elsewhere (*In Search of Philosophic Understanding*, 1965), it is to be regretted that he has
not attempted the more comprehensive treatment of the philosophy of religion that he is undoubtedly capable of. William Capi-
tan's recent *Philosophy of Religion, An Introduction* (New
York: Pegasus, 1972) though still preoccupied with immortality
and theism, has a refreshing breadth of interest in other forms of
religion, and also does not appear tied hand and foot to alleged
axioms of contemporary philosophy.

A more comprehensive and in many ways more satisfying
approach both to religion and philosophy can be found in a
number of older works that have now almost universally fallen
into disuse. Some of these, written around the turn of the present century, stand under the influence of (German) evolutionary idealism, but they at least attempt to deal with the broad
phenomenon of religion, though they usually arrive at Christianity as the highest product of religious evolution, and so as having a special place and truth. Some of them devote considerable
attention to important questions now totally overlooked in this
connection: the dialectical relationship between religion and
culture, religion and art, religion and thought, between ethical
and mystical religion, and such noteworthy topics as value-
theory and purpose in life. Harald Höffding's *The Philosophy of
Religion* (London: Macmillan, 1906) illustrates an unusual
breadth of mind, both in philosophic speculation and in interest
in diverse forms of the religious phenomenon. He establishes at
the beginning that "a philosophy of religion must not start from
any ready-made philosophical system" for its work will be most
productive when it is understood as a "process of philosophiz-
ing" in the most general sense. He acknowledges the difficulties
of the questions about truth and meaning as applied to religion,
but wonders "whether it is, after all, of the first necessity that a
solution should be found." He is interested in understanding the
phenomenon, and he consistently calls upon a broad range of
religious forms to provide data for reflection.

George Trumbull Ladd's *The Philosophy of Religion* (New
York: Scribner's, 1909, 2 vols.) is also generally excellent in its
breadth of scope. Alfred Caldecott's *The Philosophy of Religion*

in England and America (London: Methuen, 1901, 2 vols.) is a similarly comprehensive endeavor, as is Archibald Bowman's *Studies in the Philosophy of Religion* (London: Macmillan, 1938, 2 vols.). Johannes Hessen's *Religionsphilosophie* (Essen, 1948), though quite conservative, gives more attention to general axiology and some of the other issues mentioned above than we have seen in many works since. C. J. Ducasse's *A Philosophical Scrutiny of Religion* (New York: Ronald Press, 1953) maintains a view over the broad sweep of the phenomenon of religion, and refuses to be exclusively preoccupied with one philosophical view or method, though it comes out somewhat haphazard and unsystematic. The commonest defect of the older style works is that the truth question, and especially the meaning question, in regard to language, is bracketed out. The defect of most present works is an exclusive concentration on them. As Gilbert Ryle has observed, "preoccupation with the theory of meaning could be described as the occupational disease of twentieth century Anglo-Saxon and Austrian philosophy."

2. In regard to method, Whitehead writes, for instance: "When the word *proof* has been uttered, the next notion to enter the mind is halfheartedness. Unless proof has produced self-evidence and thereby rendered itself unnecessary, it has issued in a second-rate state of mind, producing action devoid of understanding. Self-evidence is the basic fact on which all greatness supports itself." "In philosophical writings proof should be at a minimum. The whole effort should be to display the self-evidence of basic truths, concerning the nature of things and their connection. . . . Philosophy, in any proper sense of the term, cannot be proved. . . . . Philosophy is either self-evident, or it is not philosophy. The attempt of any philosophic discourse should be to produce self-evidence. Of course it is impossible to achieve any such aim. But nonetheless, all inference in philosophy is a sign of that imperfection which clings to all human endeavor. The aim of philosophy is sheer disclosure." (*Modes of Thought*, Ch. 3)

1. Language

The fish trap exists because of the fish; once you've gotten the fish, you can forget the trap. The rabbit snare exists because of the rabbit; once you've gotten the rabbit, you can forget the snare. Words exist because of meaning; once you've gotten the meaning, you can forget the words. Where can I find a man who has forgotten words, so I can have a word with him?
— Chuang Tzu

No feature of life is more familiar to us than language, yet none is more opaque. Our comprehension of the way it functions is still rudimentary. The further it is analyzed, the more complex it is found to be. We imagine we understand language because we use it readily, but our use of it is little advanced beyond the primitive, is still in many ways blundering, ineffective, and often grotesquely inadequate. To understand a person's language fully we would need to understand the person himself fully; but it is his language which is our main gateway to his person. His language is more directly accessible than his thoughts. Accessibility is the point of language, and its great advantage. Deceptive though it is, it gives us a place to start. The language that religions use provides us with a point of departure for understanding them, an initial access to the way they work. The question, how do religions function, can be usefully asked first therefore as, how does religious language function.

Of the many forms that utterance takes, the statement, and especially the assertion, is particularly accessible to investigation. It can be subjected to tests of logic, for example, and its truth-value can be questioned, which is not the case with exclamations or imperatives. If we can discover how religious assertions function, we are likely to make some progress towards understanding how religions function. An assertion is a statement of alleged fact. Such statements play a role of fundamental importance in the religions of man.

Judaism as a religion is based on such assertions as that Moses led the Hebrew people out of Egypt, and that he received the Torah for them from God. For the believing Jew these are not matters of detached interest, they are the foundation on which everything else in his religion rests. The same is true of the Islamic assertion that God revealed the Koran to Mohammed, and that Mohammed is the last and greatest of the prophets. Similarly, Christianity informs us that Jesus of Nazareth rose from the dead, that there are three persons in God, that there is a final judgment, and an eternal life. The scriptures of Hinduism tell us that ultimate reality is one, that individuality is an illusion, that the deepest depth of the soul of man, the Atman, is identical with the Absolute, Brahman, that there is such a thing as reincarnation. *In each case a set of assertions gives a basis to the religion.*

That is to say, a set of alleged *facts* is considered to form the basis of the religion. The facts asserted are of two very different kinds. Some are matters of history, events which it is believed have taken place in the past, or will take place at some time in the future, such as the exodus of the Jews, the resurrection of Jesus, the enlightenment of the Buddha, or the general resurrection of mankind from the dead. Others assert metaphysical facts, such as that there exists one God, or one God in three persons, that Atman is identical with Brahman, that multiplicity is an illusion. Although we do not usually refer to assertions like these as "facts," still a religious tradition considers them to be so, that is, actually existing, objective states of affairs, true in themselves, quite apart from whether they have any effect on the individual. In this sense, religious convictions are considered to be convictions about the most important facts.

There is a distinction between the form or appearance of a statement and its function.

We can make a statement for the primary purpose of pointing out an objective matter of fact, without any suggestion that the fact makes a significant difference to us personally. These may be called "factitive" statements.

By contrast, we can make a statement for the purpose of indicating a significant difference which we believe is made to us by some state of affairs. These may be called "importative" statements, that is, statements expressing importance, or, in a special sense, "meaning." To designate the specific content of an importative statement, the (old English) noun "importancy" may be used, if it does not seem too cumbersome. It is possible for a statement to have the form or appearance of a factitive statement, and yet function as an importative one.

To describe a statement as factitive is not to imply that the statement is true, or even that it could possibly be true, but only that the person making it is not making it primarily to express a significant alteration in his own condition.

Two women are out window-shopping, and one, pointing to a dress that had looked green from a distance, remarks, "This dress is blue." It is a detached observation, made out of curiosity, and she passes on, her personal situation unaffected.

But suppose she is going to be a bridesmaid at a wedding and she has ordered a yellow dress from Christian Dior for the occasion, because the color suits her hair and fits what the bride is wearing. When it arrives and she opens the box, with its $2500 price tag, she utters the sentence, "This dress is blue." Although the verbal formulation of the statement is the same, its function is notably different. In the second case numerous substitutes are imaginable which would scarcely occur in the first. She is not making a detached observation out of curiosity; she is expressing a significant difference she believes is made to her own condition. The utterance has the form or appearance of a factitive statement, but it functions as an importative one.

While scientific assertions belong in the first group, and many philosophical ones, religious assertions belong in the second; even though they may have the appearance of stating facts, as in doctrinal statements, prayers, etc., nevertheless they function as statements of importancy or "meaning" in the sense mentioned. Statements like "there exists a supreme being," or "Moses led the Hebrew people out of Egypt," taken as the factitive assertions they appear to be, are not religious statements at all. Taken as they stand, the first is a metaphysical assertion, the second a historical one. They become religious only when they function as importative statements.

The evidence for this thesis, if evidence is needed, is not far to seek. What reason does a religious person, as distinct from a historian or philosopher, have for asserting such things, that there exists a supreme being, that the inmost soul is identical with Brahman, that God revealed the Koran to Mohammed? It is not curiosity, historical or metaphysical, that moves him. It is a conviction that in some way his own condition is personally affected. This alone is the source of his interest in them. So there exists, or does not exist, a supreme being. So what? What difference does that make to me? Unless the supreme being in question is of such a kind that my personal situation would be affected by him, I may have a metaphysical curiosity about him in odd moments, but I have no religious interest. The God of the deists is not capable of being an object of religious concern.

It is a particularly interesting feature of importancies that different facts can yield the same importancy, "make the same difference." To come back to the bridesmaid with the blue dress, it is actually a matter of complete indifference to her that the dress is precisely blue. It might just as well be pink or purple, so long as it is not the color she wanted. A green dress with red dots would make exactly the same difference to her as the blue one. Within a certain spectrum, to be discussed later, the facts may change considerably, yet have the same importance. It may be a matter for argument whether a man died from hypertension or hypoglycemia; so far as the man himself is concerned, the difference is the same. He is dead.

The religions of mankind have a remarkable power to adjust their factitive beliefs. Christians long believed it to be a matter of religious faith that the world was made in six days. When this was discovered to be scientifically unlikely, it was decided that "day" in Hebrew (*yom*) could mean a very long time, rather than twenty-four hours. Finally the biblical account was interpreted as a poetic rendering of the general "fact" of creation.

If we were to ask an adherent of the Jewish faith about the exodus of the Hebrew people from Egypt under Moses, he would be likely to assert that this historical fact was of great importance to him. But suppose we were able to put before him good historical evidence that the event known as the Exodus actually took place over a number of years, in different groups of people, so that Moses could be the leader of only one of them, whose religion was subsequently adopted by the others, what will be the reaction of the adherent of the Jewish faith? Will he give up his religion? It is possible, but it is more likely that he will say the fact remains that God revealed the Law to Moses, and that's what counts. If we carried the argument further, and we could prove that the figure of Moses was a later creation, say of the ninth century BCE, to provide a historical focus of unity for the Hebrew tribes, will he now give up his religion? Again, possibly; but more likely he will declare: Well, I know what it means to be a Jew, and for me the Jewish religion bears within itself the marks of a divine origin; if you wish to say that the story of Moses is a poetic expression of this reality, that's all right. The divine sanction of his religion is maintained, and that is what matters to him. He has thus preserved the importancy, the meaning of his religion to his own satisfaction. But he has come a long way in his factitive beliefs.

There are different sorts of differences. A difference can be made to my physical, financial, or mental state. We need to ask more closely, what sort of difference is made in my condition by a religious statement?

In appropriate circumstances, "This dress is blue" translates into "I am angry." It expresses an alteration in an emotional condition. The statement is emotionally significant. This was the sort of significance which the logical positivists attributed to religious statements: the assertion "God is good" is expressive of a feeling of happiness or contentment, for example.

Or an assertion may express an intention to act in a certain way. If someone says to me, "Let's rob the corner bank tomorrow," and I reply, "That's a good idea," my response, though in form an assertion of value in regard to his mental activity, need not be a detached observation, but may express a momentous decision to undertake a rapid and only slightly hazardous means of acquiring wealth. If the action decided on is being looked at from the point of its morality, then the statement is "ethically significant." Following R. B. Braithwaite, numerous analytic philosophers still seem to consider that this is the way religious statements function. The statement, "God is love," is equivalent to "I intend to act in a loving way."

But it is also possible for the difference made to be of a cognitive character, that is, to lie in a perception regarding the condition of the speaker. The statement, "Mr. Nixon was elected President of the United States," uttered by a historian or reporter, has the form, and perhaps the function, of a factitive assertion. Uttered by George McGovern, it might be presumed to express primarily a perception concerning his own condition.

This type of statement expresses not an emotion, nor an intention to act in a certain way, but a perception, a perception about his condition; but what sort of perception is this?

The question, what difference does it make, was given a special philosophical significance by Charles Sanders Peirce, the founder of American pragmatism. Peirce suggested it be used as a tool to obtain clarity in metaphysical statements, as a criterion to judge their usefulness. But, as observed, there are different sorts of differences, and the sort of difference Peirce was looking for is very different from the one that applies in the matter of religion. The difference Peirce and William James required is one in the realm of sense-perception. For a metaphysical assertion to be worth making, there must be some way in which our *sense-experience* would be different if the assertion was not true; for example, the type of experience we have when we attempt to verify a theory in physics or chemistry by seeing something in a microscope or on a measuring instrument. This also seems to be what R. B. Braithwaite demands when he says that for religious assertions to be cognitively significant, they would have to make some observable difference to our experience.

But in addition to sense perception in the ordinary use of the term, where we see, hear, touch, taste, or smell something, there is another type of perception which consists in seeing a pattern in things where we had not seen one before, although the observable sense experience remains the same. For example, I look at a lot of dots on a sheet of paper, and after ten minutes I suddenly see a face there. Or I enter a barn and see a lump in the corner, and my companion says to me, "That is a rabbit," and then I *see* that it looks like a rabbit. Two men look at a sunset; one of them says; "Isn't that beautiful!" The other says, "I don't see it."

A related type of perception, though nonvisual, is at work when a psychologist looks at the observable phenomena of human behavior and sees in them a pattern corresponding to Freud's theories, while another, looking at exactly the same activities, sees a pattern which corresponds to behaviorist theory.

The question whether this latter type of perception can be validated or verified is another matter, and will be dealt with subsequently. For the moment it may suffice to point out this other type of perception, and to suggest that it is within this realm that religious assertions belong, as importative statements of a perceptional character.

The religious man then sees something differently. What does he see? I think we must say that he sees "life" differently. That is to say, it is not a question of seeing an isolated event in a different light; it is a matter of how he interprets his overall experience. It is, in some sense, the totality of his life-experience, taken as a totality, which is interpreted.

If Jesus of Nazareth was God, then our interpretation of human life must change. We cannot justifiably go on doing business as usual. If the Koran was revealed by God to Mohammed, then we need to rethink our overall approach to things, not just to this or that. If our impression that we exist as distinct individuals is an illusion, then our conception of what life as a whole is all about must be altered. The interpretation which we place on the totality of experience is at stake in these things. A religion presents us with a vision of life.

Phrases like "a vision of life" or "the meaning of life" are vague. It would be helpful if we could arrive at a clearer notion of what such a thing is. It would be especially helpful if we could discover the elements that go to make it up. In point of fact it seems that we can distinguish a number of components that comprise a vision of life.

In the first place, there is a statement, explicit or implied, about the principal experienced *problem* man faces in life. What is the chief obstacle to human hope? Usually there will be an assertion that some particular aspect of experience constitutes a main difficulty.

It is possible, for example, to experience the world of Nature as the principal problem in life. In primitive cultures and religions this tends to be an unreflected assumption, where human existence is obviously dependent on the grass, the sheep and cattle, the crops, the sun shining and the rain falling at the proper time. In Chinese thinking Nature (the unity of Heaven, Earth, and man) has been grasped explicitly and profoundly as the source of man's existence, and the framework of his life. In the reflective Taoism of the *Tao Te Ching* and *Chuang Tzu* it is man's lack of harmony with Nature that is responsible for his woes. Man is not the measure of Nature, he is part of it and is to be understood in terms of it; Nature is the measure of man. If Nature is supreme, to be out of harmony with it is disaster. This is man's chief problem in life, and the experience of it is the main obstacle to his hope—though Chinese literature is not given, in general, to expatiating on the problematic or darker side of life.

(This conception of man's chief difficulty in life is not confined to Taoism, as might seem; it also applies to Confucianism. The Confucian concern with the right ordering of society, and even the neo-Confucian concentration on "the moral mind," exist within an overarching framework which sees society itself as part of nature. Not that Confucianism develops the "romantic" attitude to nature that characterizes the Taoist poets, but it develops within a characteristically Chinese conception of man and society which sees both in terms of what is possible within the given framework of Nature. If *Chuang Tzu* and the *Tao Te Ching* deal explicitly with the problem of how to live in harmony with nature, the Confucian tradition deals with the problem of social structures, but social structures themselves are experienced as a problem precisely insofar as they are not a deliberate creation of man's, but are part of the intractable soil of our lives which we call "nature.")

A very different conception of man's chief problem in life is that it lies in the experience of suffering as such, not in nature but in man himself: that part of man which suffers, the suffering self. It is this conviction which lies at the roots of the religions of Indian origin, Buddhism, Hinduism, Jainism. What would you do if you found yourself in the middle of the Sahara with a toothache? That is perhaps not too far from the problem which these religions deal with. The Buddha expressed it clearly: the whole of life is suffering:

"birth is painful, old age is painful, sickness is painful, death is painful, sorrow, lamentation, dejection and despair are painful." The Brahmanist Svetasvatara Upanishad utters the same view:

> "Forgetting his oneness with thee,
> Bewildered by his weakness,
> Full of sorrow is man."

To be a human being is necessarily and inevitably to suffer. I am my own worst enemy. Not Nature—Nature would have no power to hurt me if I did not let it. It is I who allow it to overwhelm me, who give it its power over me. For the Hindu, the Jain, and the Buddhist man's principal problem is himself, his distinct, individual, material existence, which lays him open and vulnerable to the painfulness and restrictions of finitude.

Another possible conception of man's principal problem in life, and again a very different one from the preceding, is that it consists in my fellowman, more accurately in my relationships with my fellowmen. In this case the chief obstacle to hope is not nature, nor myself, but you, that is, my relationship with you. Here man is not viewed as a part of nature, but as a person who stands uniquely over against nature and in contrast to it. The distinctive notion of personhood is highly developed in such a view. Correspondingly, man's outstanding hindrance in life is the experience of the sheer nastiness, the hardheartedness of human beings towards each other. Acute awareness of injustice lies at the root of the ethical religions, and their most fundamental conviction is that justice must be done some day. This view characterizes the religions of Semitic origin—Judaism, Christianity, and Islam, and also Zoroastrianism. Since it is in this realm that moral notions apply, these religions have developed appropriate moral conceptions, such as sin, guilt, conscience, repentance, and forgiveness much more fully than the Chinese or Indian. (Reference to Confucianism as primarily an ethic is only justifiable if "ethic" is understood in the most general sense as referring to a pattern of desirable activity.)

This one problem, of the relationships between people, can be experienced in a variety of ways, depending largely on the prevailing stage of cultural development.

In the primitive society of nomads and agriculturists-with-difficulty of ancient Persia, the problem posed itself in the simple terms of "the good" versus "the wicked," the "war of the sons of light against the sons of darkness," to adopt a later but appropriate title. When a certain degree of sophistication has been achieved, this naive dualism is at least partly overcome, and the possibility can be considered that "wickedness" may be present in me too and not only in the "enemy."

In the tribal society of Israel, the problem presented itself in terms of tribal relationships with the rest of mankind. The period of the development of classic biblical Judaism, after 538 BC, is marked by the ambiguity of the necessity of ethnic unity as a condition of survival and restoration on the one hand, and the exilic and postexilic experience of the larger world beyond, the unity of the Persian world empire, and later of the Greco-Roman world. Judaism has never escaped from this tension; it has never been simply a tribal religion, but it has also never been able to become universal in scope. Its experience of the problem of relationships between people has consequently been marked by the same tension; relationships with mankind in general are important, but relationships within the ethnic group have a special importance.

The step to a fully universal scope was made with Christianity, and subsequently followed in Islam. In each case the problem which the religion is designed to tackle is that of the relationships between people in general. However, the religion's ability to deal with the problem is conditional on people's joining the religion, so that on the one hand there is a consciousness of the special importance of relationships between members of the religion, and on the other there is a drive to incorporate the whole of mankind within the religion. Even so, the problem of interpersonal relationships which Christianity is designed to deal with is not identical with that of Islam, since Islam's emphasis on the fulfillment of a law flows from a concern for the public aspect of the problem, while Christianity's attachment to an individual savior figure identified with a historical person is an expression of a greater emphasis on private relationships between individuals. Christianity is peculiarly concerned with the problem of men's inner attitudes towards one another, rather than their external activity. The decisive thing is a person's intentions.

Another possible conception of man's principal problem in life is that it consists in the repressive and exploitative character of social structures. This is the conviction with which Marxism begins. Although social structures are created by people, once created they tend to take on a life of their own and they then react on the people sustaining them, remoulding and refashioning their creators. Men are the prisoners of situations they are themselves the authors of. This problem may be felt as an economic one, as in classical Marxism, the division of society into exploiters and exploited; or it may be experienced more as an existential problem, the fact that my identity as a person is created by the people around me, rather than by myself; or it may be viewed primarily as a case of social repression in terms of general power rather than of class economics alone. In any of these cases, the attitude of individual people to one an-

other, whether good or bad, is not the problem. It is irrelevant whether a person is "well-intentioned" or not. The
decisive thing is the role he acts out in society, the social
function he performs. If he is in fact a member of an ex-
ploiting or repressive class, no amount of "goodwill" can
rectify the situation. He must either change his public activities or else run the risk of elimination.

Another conception of man's principal problem is that it
lies in the absurdity of life. This view has been expressed
with impressive force in Western literature especially since
World War II. Life is meaningless and futile, nonsensical,
preposterous and monstrous. This conviction is not the
product of a set of reasonings: it is an experience; an experience which renders hope ridiculous. Religious systems
which offer man hope blind him to the reality of life, and
deprive him of the limited pleasure he might have had a
chance to enjoy.

In the actual course of life, unreflected upon, no doubt
all these things mentioned, and others, nature, suffering,
interpersonal relationships, the repressive character of social structures, and sheer absurdity, are experienced all together in a vague and undistinguished way, as constituting
the obstacle to human hope. But it is proper to speak of an
interpretation of life only when the elements of experience
are distinguished, when priorities are assigned, and when
the vision is structured.

How are we to decide what does in fact constitute man's
principal problem in life? This question will be considered
later, but it seems likely that no one principal problem may
be valid forever. What is experienced as the chief obstacle
to hope must be assumed to vary with the cultural situation, that is, from culture to culture, and within the one
culture as it develops from less to more advanced forms. As
a culture becomes more sophisticated, so do its problems.

To experience distinctly, especially in a psychological way, the repressive character of social structures as the principal problem in life, already requires a relatively advanced level of civilization; it is a rich man's disease.

The second component we find in interpretations of life is the proposal of what may be called, by a slight stretch of language, an "empirical ideal." This is a state of affairs, thought to be experienceable, that will constitute the solution of the principal experienced problem of life. It solves the problem by being its logical contrary.

If the problem is man's lack of harmony with nature, this already contains within it the assertion that the most desirable state of affairs is one in which man achieves harmony with nature. This is the ideal proposed to us in the *Tao Te Ching.* Harmony with nature means fitting in with nature, not trying to impose one's desires on it, not treating it with violence, but allowing it to give expression to itself in one's attitudes, actions, and being.

Nature in this sense is not something distinct from man; man is part of nature. A state of harmony with nature is a state where harmony prevails within nature itself. The first characteristic of such a state would be that the universe would function properly. Human life would work. Things would run smoothly. From one point of view this would bring a great increase in power. People in harmony with nature would be capable of doing all sorts of things now impossible to them. The knife used in accordance with nature does not blunt. But this power is not violent; violence is a distortion of nature. It is a power out of weakness, not needing the crudity of force to achieve what is needful, either with men or with things. This power is simply the outward reflection of true wisdom, which understands the universe not merely theoretically but directly, because it is profoundly in tune with it.

If man's principal problem is considered to be the experience of suffering, one conceivable remedy would be to disengage, if possible, that portion of the self which suffers. This would mean an inner rearrangement, an interior adjustment of the mind, so that the suffering is no longer experienced, and therefore ceases to be suffering. If this could be achieved, it would solve the problem of pain in general, whereas attempts to remove the external cause of pain, for example by the use of medicine, will only work from case to case, and a new remedy has to be discovered for each occasion. The latter is the way of science and technology, to proceed piece by piece, trying to overcome one individual problem after another. The former, the way of interior mental adjustment, is the solution offered by the Hindu, the Jain, and the Buddhist, each in his own way.

Early Buddhism was clear and explicit that it was offering this remedy. In the Buddha's *Sermon at Benares*, after it has been stated that the experience of suffering is man's chief problem in life, and that the cause of suffering lies within man himself, in his inordinate desires, "the craving for passion, the craving for existence, the craving for non-existence," we are told that the remedy lies in detaching oneself from oneself, so that the portion of the self which suffers is let go and disengaged.

> "Now this, monks, is the noble truth of the cessation of pain, the cessation without a remainder of craving, the abandonment, forsaking, release, non-attachment."

While Buddhism treats the problem directly on the practical level, and deliberately abstains from metaphysical speculations, Hinduism in its early reflective stage, as represented in the Upanishads, deals with the problem by putting forward a profound, mystical, and metaphysical system: the doctrine that all things are one, that multiplicity is an illusion, that at the core of its being every entity is identical with every other entity, and thus there exists only one real Being, hidden from us now by the veil of our senses. In its extreme metaphysical form this doctrine is associated preeminently with the particular school of *advaita vedanta*, and the name of Shankara. But anyone familiar with India knows that in a more general sense this view is at the heart of Indian culture. Shankara simply gave logical rigor to what India on the whole has thought. Suffering belongs to the world of experience, which is an illusion. It is overcome when we realize our fundamental unity with the One. This One, Brahman, is identical with the true Self of every human being. It is immortal, not subject to suffering and death. Therefore our search for release is a search for our true Self, which lies beyond all death and pain.

> Brahman alone is—nothing else is.
> He dwells deep within the heart.
> He is the Lord of time, past and future.
> Having attained him, one fears
> no more, he is the immortal Self.
> —*Katha Upanishad*

If man's principal problem in life is conceived to be his relationships with other human beings, then it is natural that the ideal remedy for his condition will be seen in a state of affairs where ethical wickedness is overcome and men treat one another properly. Where sufficient sophistication has been reached to perceive that ethical wickedness is just as likely to be present in myself as in others, the removal of past failures, that is, the forgiveness of sin, will be a prerequisite.

This condition of things, where offenses have been forgiven, and men treat one another rightly, may be designated "ethical salvation." In Zoroastrian literature it is given physical and metaphysical embodiment in the

"House of Song," in the New Testament in "the Reign of God," in the Koran in "paradise." These images of "heaven" frequently give a first appearance of being simply a place or state of happiness, but closer examination shows that they have strongly moral features. They are the triumph of moral goodness over moral evil. They are animated by the conviction that one day justice must be done. The "House of Song" represents the victory of the good over the wicked, assigned to the "House of the Lie." When the "Reign of God" is described, it is in terms of the attitudes of people toward one another, as in Matthew 25. The Koranic "paradise," though pictured in very physical terms, is for those who "give sustenance to the poor man, the orphan, and the captive." It is for the "righteous" who "dread the far-spread terrors of Judgment Day," while "for the wrong-doers He has prepared a grievous punishment" (cf. Surah 76).

It can be suggested that the idea of a personal God, of a judgment, and of a "Reign of God" to come naturally lead a religion to emphasize personal ethics. No doubt that is possible. The suggestion being made here, however, is that, considering the way these religions function in the lives of people, the reverse is the case. It is the strongly personal *experience* of evil, that is, of evil as a matter of the attitude of persons toward one another, of the "good" versus the "wicked," that requires the ideas of a judgment, and so of a personal God and a "Kingdom of God." When the notion is overcome that it is possible to divide mankind into the "good" on the one hand and the "wicked" on the other, when, for example, the conviction grows, as it must with increased sophistication, that both of these elements are to be found mixed in all people, and no clear-cut ethical separation of mankind is possible, the ethical religions begin to be in danger. The threat becomes more serious still when the inspiration of human behavior comes to be considered rather a matter of psychology than of ethics.

The details of the concrete embodiments and locations of ethical salvation vary considerably. Sometimes it is expected to occur within history, as its final and crowning epoch, as in late Jewish and early Christian apocalypticism, or, in a much more refined version, in the evolutionary theory of Teilhard de Chardin. Sometimes the two notions are combined, as in the Christian doctrine of heaven, to be entered by souls immediately after death, and the day of judgment, bringing the end of history.

Where man's principal problem is identified as the repressive character of social structures, the ideal remedy will be a state of affairs where social structures are no longer repressive, whether economically, psychologically, or politically, according to the more precise definition of the problem. The classless society of Marxism and recent freedom movements in the United States exemplify this type of solution.

If our principal problem is the absurdity of life, one remedy, at least a means of dealing with the problem, consists in having the strength to acknowledge the absurdity and not flinch before it, to stick it out and refuse to lose heart, though realizing that hope is vain. Whether this can be considered an interpretation of life may be questioned. An interpretation is a perception, or a claim to perception, of a pattern in some sense intelligible, which is rejected by definition in this case. But, paradoxically, the act of declaring life absurd is one way of rendering it intelligible. When I can say of something that it is absurd, I have placed it in a category where I can understand it!

The third major component of an interpretation of life consists in a statement about the realization of the ideal solution. This itself seems to contain two chief elements.

There is an estimate of the *chances* of the solution being realized. It may be that the ideal solution remains an ideal, as in the Confucian tradition which never nourished high hopes that the golden age would return. Or it may be that it is up to us whether the solution is attained or not: it is possible, but there is no guarantee. This would be true in general of the Buddhist outlook. Or it may be that there is a guarantee, an assurance, that one day the ideal solution will actually come about. This is the case with the Semitic religions' expectation of "the reign of God," and Marxism's classless society.

This element, the degree of certainty with which final realization of the ideal is expected, is quite essentially crucial for any interpretation of life. The issue that has priority over all other issues is whether human life has a purpose, a goal, built into it, that is, whether it already possesses of itself a directedness towards an ultimate realization, or whether in itself it is purposeless. In the first case life has "meaning" of itself, and the goals we set for ourselves will need to be in harmony with that meaning. In the second case it is we who must give meaning to life by setting our own goals, and we have no criteria to fall back on other than ourselves and what we create.

If it is expected with assurance that the ideal state of affairs will one day be realized, then the first of these options is implied: life has a goal built into it. If final realization of the ideal state of things is not expected with certainty, then there is no conception of life having a goal, a directedness, of itself; it is up to me to make my life "meaningful" by setting up my own "project" and working towards it. This is the great gulf between the religions of Semitic and those of Indian and Chinese origin. The phrase, "the meaning of life," can be used in these two very different contexts only by analogy.

To those raised under the influence of a Semitic religion, this certainty about important things to come tends to seem a constituent part of religion itself; difficulty is felt in even calling a tradition lacking it, like Confucianism, a "religion."

A distinction must be drawn between public or objective realization of the ideal, and the private participation of the individual in it. Public realization of the ideal may be guaranteed, and the participation of the individual highly doubtful, as in many forms of the Semitic religions. The participation of the individual in whatever constitutes "salvation" is usually dependent on his fulfillment of certain conditions.

This distinction between public and individual salvation explains at least partly the distinct roles played by the ideas of God and the savior in the Semitic religions. If we ask, what does God actually do that would make some experienceable difference, and what does the savior do that would make some experienceable difference to that, it appears that God is the one who brings about the public or objective realization of the ideal, while the savior is one who in a special way makes it possible for the individual to participate in that, renders it personally accessible to him. Notions like the *kami* of Shintoism, or the Melanesian *mana*, are assertions that there exists a power capable of solving man's problems with nature, but without any guarantee that it will actually do so for the individual.

Secondly, there is a statement about the location or availity of the resources needed to realize the solution. One option here consists in the conviction that man possesses within himself the resources he needs to achieve the goal. Man can and must save himself. This outlook may be termed "Pelagian," and characterizes early Theravada Buddhism, and much of Islam. The Buddha could tell his disciples that there is no light to help them other than that which they carry within themselves, but that is sufficient. "Be ye lamps unto yourselves."

The contrasting conviction is that man does not possess the needed resources within himself. He cannot save himself. If he is to be saved, he needs help from outside. This outlook may be termed "saviorist," and has characterized much of Mahayana Buddhism and Christianity. Another alternative is that the resources for the attainment of the goal are contained in nature, the view of Taoism, and also, in its own way, ("the world-historical process") of Marxism.

The three elements mentioned so far are components of the *theoria*, the theoretical aspect of an interpretation of life. This does not rest in itself, but entails, and is entailed by, action. A religion holds out a vision and the vision points out a path to be followed. An interpretation of life implies a way of life.

A vision of life does not usually exist in people's minds with the clarity of theoretical structure outlined here; like all vision, it will have at any given moment a particular focus, and surrounding that a large, vague field which is intuited rather than seen. But the theoretical elements of the vision are implied in the way of life it proposes, since it is a function of them, and the effectiveness of a religion depends on the adoption of its way of life. There is a tendency therefore for religions to lay quantitatively greater stress on the way of life they propose than on the theoretical considerations underlying it.

Two men in winter look at the side of a mountain covered with snow. What do they see? One says: It is cold, hard, and unfriendly, a man might perish there. The other says: The snow is glistening in the sun, look at the soft contours of the rise; and the slope would make a great run for a pair of skis.

One man looks at life, and says: He who knows does not speak; he who speaks does not know.

Another says: Life is suffering. We suffer when we are born, and we suffer when we die. But we suffer because of ourselves, our foolish desires. Let us seek release, abandonment, forsaking, the extinction of craving.

Another says: This life is an illusion. The Imperishable alone is the Real. We are in misery because we have forgotten our oneness with Him who does not die. But truly we are one with Him, and with one another, and with all things, and He is our joy.

Another says: Your hands are full of blood. You cry peace, peace, and there is no peace. Every man is an enemy to his neighbor. The good man perishes, and no one lays it to heart. Justice must be done! Share your bread with the hungry, and bring the poor into your house!

The difference between these reactions is not a matter of metaphysics or of history, or even of ethics. It is a difference of *vision*.

NOTE

The *inadequacy* of language about the ultimate reality, whether conceived theistically or nontheistically, has long been a commonplace with religious writers. In the Upanishads (Brihadaranyaka) Brahman can be described neither as this nor that— *neti, neti.* In China the *Tao Te Ching* or *Lao Tzu*, probably to be dated about the fourth century B.C., shows a profound grasp of the problem: The Tao that can be uttered is not the real Tao. Comparably a theist says, the God that you understand is not the real God. "My thoughts are not your thoughts, and your ways are not my ways" (Isaiah 55). The Indian Buddhist Nagarjuna (c. A.D. 100) uses reason to show the inadequacy of reason, and by implication of language, to express the true Buddhanature. A contrasting response to the problem of uttering the unutterable is Augustine's cry in his *Confessions* (A.D. 399):

Woe to them that speak not of You at all, since those who say
most are but dumb.

A highly developed method for dealing with the inadequacy
of language about God was put forward by an unknown Byzan-
tine writer of the fifth century pseudonomously called Dionysius
the Areopagite. In two works *The Divine Names* and *The Mystical Theology* he suggests three levels of discourse about God:
one, in which we affirm of God those perfections we partially
experience in the world, e.g., wisdom, power, goodness. On this
first level we say "God is good," for example. But since the
notion "good" is derived from our finite experience, it cannot
apply, in any sense that we can give it, to God. Therefore we
must also say: "God is not good," i.e., he is not good in any
sense I can give to the word "good." But we cannot and do not
wish to remain on this level of mere negation. It is not enough to
say of God that he is not wise, powerful, or good. Therefore we
must transcend and negate even this negation. This transcen-
dence or negation of the negation has implications for the first
level: If we wish to say: God is good, we can legitimately do so
only *via eminentiae*: the term must be taken as if it had a higher
meaning that went beyond our experience.

The "negative theology" of Pseudo-Dionysius was taken up by
Maximus the Confessor (died 662), and propagated in western
Europe by Duns Scotus Erigena in the ninth century. Its significance was acknowledged by Thomas Aquinas (Summa Theol. I,
q. 13, art. 1, ad 1), but it was submerged in his doctrine of the
analogy of being, which made meaningful speech about God
possible by analogy (cf. I, q. 13, art. 5, c.a.).

The question of the adequacy of God-language was always
also a question about its meaningfulness, but in the present
century the question of meaning has become paramount. The
early verification principle of the logical positivists (a term applied initially to the so-called Vienna Circle, and subsequently to
adherents such as A. J. Ayer in the English-speaking world who
diffused a related outlook) laid it down that a statement has
meaning only to the extent that it can be verified. Later this was
modified to: the meaning of a statement is given by the method
of its verification. (Ayer, *Language, Truth and Logic*, 1936, and
the collection edited by him, *Logical Positivism*, 1959). This left
room for different kinds of meanings, based on different sorts of
verifications, but both forms of the principle excluded "meta-

physical" assertions, and so all assertions about God, from having meaning.

Ludwig Wittgenstein's early work, the *Tractatus Logicophilosophicus* (1921) presented a view akin to that of the logical positivists, though less concerned with scientific method as a model, and more with language. "The whole sense of the book might be summed up in the following words: what can be said at all can be said clearly, and what we cannot talk about we must pass over in silence" (Author's Preface). Some obscure references to "the mystical," however, left in doubt the status of the religious for Wittgenstein.

In his later *Philosophical Investigations*, published posthumously (1953), he abandoned his previous view of language as a uniform activity, in favor of a variety of "language-games" —differing, self-coherent modes of using language in life-contexts and of behaving with language. In this view the meaning of a particular piece of language is at least often given by its *use*. Wherever language is used, then, it will have *some* meaning, and the trick is to discover in what language-game it is being used, for this tells us how it is used.

An imaginative application of related views to theistic language was made by John Wisdom, in a deservedly famous paper "Gods." He suggests that the function of language about divinities is to convey a way of looking at life.

Wittgenstein's and Wisdom's treatments of perception and "seeing as . . ." are indicated more fully in the note to Chapter 7. For the moment the first two chapters of the present essay can be taken as an attempt to develop more systematically some implications of Wisdom's suggestion mentioned here, to specify more closely what sort of language is used to convey a way of looking at life (importative rather than factitive), and what structure a "way of looking at life" could be said to have (e.g., the recognition of a problematic dimension, assertion of a corresponding ideal, expectation regarding the certainty of actualization of the ideal, and its extent).

"Importance" and its distinction from "matter-of-fact" are elegantly elaborated by Alfred North Whitehead in *Modes of Thought* (New York: Macmillan, 1938). Although his account of them differs somewhat from that given here, the present essay is probably more deeply indebted to Whitehead than to any other thinker. He defines importance as a form of interest—

"interest involving that intensity of individual feeling which leads to publicity of expression." By "interest" he refers to a quality of the object, rather than to an activity of a subject. It is the latter sense however that is central to the present essay. Notions of importance and interest apparently derived from Whitehead have been admirably developed and applied to religion by William Christian (*Meaning and Truth in Religion,* Princeton, 1964).

Whitehead's concept of "importance" is not unrelated to Martin Heidegger's *das Existenzielle.* This is the class of those things that are inwardly or personally experienced as making a difference to us. In *Being and Time* Heidegger elevated this notion to the status of a key ontological category, with its companion, *das Existenziale:* the class of the structural elements of *Dasein.* Both terms in their undifferentiating English translation "existential" have long since become popular catchwords and scarcely require elaboration here.

Early in the twentieth century a number of Christian theologians such as Romano Guardini and Karl Barth began to suggest that the doctrines of the Christian faith should be presented in such a way that the difference they made to people was emphasized, rather than their factual content. This suggestion has been given extreme form by Rudolph Bultmann, who has proposed that all merely factual elements be eliminated from the Christian Gospel, in favor of an existential interpretation of it. Programs of existential interpretation have subsequently found general favor with Christian theologians, especially Karl Rahner, Heinrich Ott and Edward Schillebeeckx, though controversy still rages over the nature and extent it should have.

None of those named went so far as to maintain that all religious assertions, not merely those of Christianity, do actually function willy-nilly as existential statements. Some such position is very nearly implicit in the works of Paul Tillich, but he did not state it explicitly.

2. Facts

"Simple," I ejaculated.

"Well, really, it can hardly be described as otherwise," said Sherlock Holmes, smiling at my surprise. "In solving a problem of this sort, the grand thing is to be able to reason backwards."

— Conan Doyle
A Study in Scarlet

It has been suggested in the previous chapter that the function of religious assertions is importative, in contrast to their frequently factitive form or appearance. They convey importance: they express a meaning in the sense of a difference believed to be made to the condition of the speaker. In form, however, they continue to be factitive; they give the appearance of asserting facts, actually existing states of affairs, often exotic ones, such as that there exists a personal God, or that everything is one. We have discovered that this appearance is deceptive, not in the sense that they tell us false facts rather than true facts, but that it is not their primary or distinctive function to tell us facts at all. They are not in the business of giving information, but of telling us how to look at life. Taking life as a totality, we should look at it this way rather than that way; rather as if someone should say to an enthusiastic but doubtful sailor faced with heavy seas, "You ought to look on this as a chance to improve your skill, rather than as a danger."

This revelation about the true and proper function of religious assertions, however, does not defuse them easily. We want to know the facts. If we are philosophical, we are curious. If we are religious, we are concerned. Religious assertions in their factitive form appear to assuage what we feel is a basic need. How can we ignore this promise? We want to know whether there is a personal God or not, whether the soul is immortal or not, whether it is really true or false that everything is one.

For the consolation of those still enmeshed in this desire for factual knowledge, it needs to be made clear that there is, after all, information of a factual kind conveyed by some religious assertions, not directly, but incidentally and in passing. The information they convey is not the distinct or determinate fact that they appear to convey, but rather a *representative* fact, which stands for a *spectrum* of acceptable facts. Further, and what for many is perhaps worse, some of the most significant information conveyed in some of the most significant religions, notably those of Semitic origin, turn out on examination to refer exclusively to the *future*. Unconditional statements about the future have a peculiar logic; they are neither true or false *now*, as Aristotle already knew. This particular piece of information may be regarded by some as disappointing, but I would like to invite them to look on it rather as curious and interesting.

Let us return to the first point, our healthy desire for distinct and determinate facts. After all, we are not to be deceived by talk of "ways of looking at things" or "interpretations" or "meanings but not facts." We know very well that you cannot have a meaning without a fact. If a difference is to be made, there must be something that makes the difference. Let those who wish rejoice in injunctions to "have a positive attitude," as the occasional billboard invites us. We are only too sadly aware that a positive attitude is only justified if there are facts to back it up. It would be worse than self-deception to have a positive attitude if there were no grounds for such a position. From the viewpoint of our Western tradition it would be positively immoral, ethically unjustifiable; we have a moral duty *not* to have a positive attitude if the facts do not warrant it. Therefore in any given situation we hold it our bounden duty to begin with the facts. Once we have the facts, we can proceed to find out what difference they will make to us.

In religion, however, this line of reasoning, otherwise so well approved, is a trap. Religions, like Sherlock Holmes, reason backwards in such matters. If we wish to get clear regarding the ultimate facts about life as a religion suggests them to us, it is a great mistake to try to discover these facts first, by some sort of independent philosophical or historical inquiry, and then deduce from them what the religion should be like and how it should look at life. That may be the way we would like to work, but it is not the way religions work. A religion begins with a vision, a way of looking at life, and then it discovers whatever ultimate facts are needed to sustain that vision. If the vision is right, if the interpretation of life is correct, it is not unreasonable to suppose that the ultimate facts it requires will be right too.

That such a modus operandi is peculiar to religion would be a naive opinion; ability to discover the facts needed to support a way of looking at things is not only a common endowment of humanity, but the effective beginning of scientific method and philosophical argument. Logical deduction is inevitably argument put in the service of a way of looking at things already opted for. This does not mean that people are not ready to change their way of looking at things when presented with a convincing argument about facts, but by the nature of the case they never begin with argument. The decision to use argument is already the expression of a particular way of looking at things. In this sense it is quite true that scientific method is an ideology, as is the critical philosophy which points that out. We urgently need a systematic method for correcting points of view and ways of looking at things, and it must be a method which can dispense with logic and scientific method, otherwise the point of view involved in using logic and scientific method can never be put in question effectively.

In politics and in courts of law we take it for granted that point of view is prior to argument, that the primary thing is the speaker's way of looking at things, and that his reasoning will be used to support that. In any speech on behalf of an institution, whether a nation or a business firm, it is inevitable not only that the argument will be determined by the point of view, but that what appears as the point of view of the individual is not even that, but one which he adopts and presents as his own because of a prior commitment to the institution. The objection raised against theology, that it is not to be taken seriously because it is defense of a *parti pris*, would hold as much and as little against any argument on behalf of any institution whatever.

In what goes beyond immediate experience, what we allow as a fact is determined by our point of view. Immediate experience has a special priority. Our ability to communicate effectively with one another about it shows that there is at least an area here which escapes the dominion of point of view. Anyone who attempts to walk directly across my sitting room will bark his shins on the slate coffee table that stolidly occupies the middle of the room. But as soon as we take a step beyond the directly observable it is our point of view that determines what shall count as a fact. Religions deal with matters of fact that go as far as possible beyond the directly observable. It is not surprising that in this realm point of view has absolute

priority. It is natural and inevitable that the overall interpretation of life will come first, and the facts of metaphysics
or history required by it will follow after.

It is not regrettable, or a lapse from the ideal, that religions work in this way. Their procedure is justifiable. We
have no direct access to a world of ultimate facts. We do
have direct access to the experience of life, and so to an
interpretation of life, an overall point of view. But the
individual rarely if ever is able to achieve a unified interpretation of life, a coherent and self-consistent point of
view. He operates rather with a bundle of partial stand-
points, with conflicting values and changing perspectives, as
he moves from one situation to another. The function performed by a religion is to bring order and unity to this
chaos, by suggesting an overall interpretation of life which
bears the marks of coherence. Elusive though it may be,
such an interpretation of life is much closer to hand for the
individual, from occasion to occasion, than any set of ultimate facts beyond the horizon of experience altogether. It is
sound and right to begin with an interpretation of life that
commends itself, and then to postulate whatever ulterior
facts it may demand—to begin with the view that life is
suffering and alienation, that our suffering selves are not
our true selves, and to conclude that there is a true Self in
which all alienation disappears, or to begin with the view
that the most important thing in life is that justice be done,
that it is intolerable that justice not be done, and to conclude therefore that there exists One who will do justice. It
is not in this transition from interpretation to fact that the
trouble lies, but in deciding which interpretation of life is
the right one. The transition itself is both logically justifiable and humanly necessary. If we are interested in ascer-
taining the ultimate facts, we might do well to travel the

same road and begin with the interpretation of our experience of life; it does not seem that there is any other road to travel to that land beyond our horizon.

This method that religions have for arriving at their factitive statements has some significant consequences. One main one is that such statements are not to be taken in the distinct and determinate form in which they appear. The fact stated by a factitive statement in religion is a representative fact. That is, it stands for all the other facts that with a little imagination might support the vision just as well. For if it is true that there cannot be a meaning without a fact, that there cannot be a difference without something that makes the difference, it is equally true that different facts can yield the same meaning, different states of affairs can make the same difference. To return to the lady who ordered the yellow dress for the wedding and on opening the box exclaims, "This dress is blue," let us imagine that her husband takes it on himself to point out that she is in error, that actually the dress is a shade of turquoise. She could be expected to reply, "Well, you idiot, so it's turquoise! That's a great help." It still isn't the color she wants. Supposing he were talking to her on the telephone after she has opened the box, and she said, "I ordered a yellow dress but they didn't send me the color I wanted." If the line then went dead and he was left wondering what color she did get, there would be two available answers: either she got some other color than yellow and it won't do, or she got a shade of yellow different from the one she wanted, but it will do. There is, then, a wide range of objective facts capable of making the undesired difference of a dress she could not wear ("any color except yellow") and also a range of facts capable of making the desired difference of a dress she could wear ("some acceptable shade of yellow").

A man goes to pick up his automobile from a garage where he had left it for what he considered minor repairs. He emerges from the shop with a bill for $150 and a strong sense of indignation. "This is outrageous. They have charged me $150—$50 for labor and $100 for parts." If his wife observes to him, "No, you've made a mistake, dear. They charged you only $50 for parts, and the $100 is for labor," he is likely to feel his point has been missed. He is still being charged more than he expected.

When we are concerned primarily with the difference made to us, the fact is of concern only insofar as it makes the difference. As a result there will always be a *spectrum* of possible facts, any one of which could bring about the difference we are concerned with.

The Roman Catholic Council of Trent defined that seven sacraments were instituted by Jesus Christ: not only baptism and the eucharist, of which there is record in the New Testament, but also confirmation and the annointing of the sick, for which there is no evidence whatever of their being instituted by Jesus. Historically speaking, it seems extremely unlikely that Jesus personally informed his apostles that confirmation and the last annointing were "sacraments," or that there were precisely seven of these. If he did, the early Christian Church forgot about it promptly, and did not remember it again till several centuries later. What is a Catholic to make of an official statement of his church like this? Following our line of argument, he would first have to ask: What is the point of the statement; what difference would it make if these ceremonies were instituted by Jesus? Perhaps the difference would be that they would have a very special significance for man's relationship to God, a significance not to be gainsaid; they would have an element of definitive seriousness. Let us suppose, however, that a person is convinced that the establishment of Christianity bears the marks of a divine act, and that such a religion as Christianity naturally expresses itself and has historically decided to express itself in certain rituals for decisive moments and aspects of a person's life. It might be expected that that would effectively give these ceremonies the same unique force for a Christian, even if in point of historical fact they were not personally instituted by Jesus.

The factitive statement that Jesus is the Son of God in a metaphysical sense is a derivation of the meaning statement that he is the savior. The Christian church arrived early at the conviction that Jesus was the savior of mankind, and for a time got along quite well on the idea that he was the Son of God in the moral or adoptional sense familiar to the Hebrew world as the factual basis for his saviorhood. The encounter with Hellenistic concern for the *eidos*, the idea or essence of a thing, led to the metaphysical conception of his sonship, and the Christian church found to its embarrassment that it apparently had two Gods. It must be maintained, however, that even in its metaphysical formulation the statement, "Jesus is the Son of God," functions in Christianity not as a metaphysical fact statement, but as a meaning statement, and the meaning it expresses may perhaps be stated summarily here as: although man cannot save himself ethically, ethical salvation is *accessible* to him.

Granted that this, or something like it, is the religious meaning of what has the form of an assertion of metaphysical fact, one would need to inquire whether it is necessary, in order to preserve the meaning that ethical salvation is available to men, to conclude that Jesus is the Son of God in the now traditional (since the fourth century) metaphysical sense, or is it possible that his relationship to God might be defined in other terms? It must be said that in principle it is possible that another set of facts could supply the same meaning and make the same difference, even if at present it is not clear to Christians what these other facts might be. Whether some other theory about the relationship of Jesus to God will prove compatible with the Christian tradition will depend on whether it is capable of yielding the same meaning, i.e., having the same importance.

The Christian community has lived for a long time on the conviction that there exists a God distinct from the world. Taken as it stands, "there exists a Supreme Being distinct from the world" is a statement of metaphysics, not of religion, a factitive statement, not an importative one. When it is used as a religious affirmation, however, it functions as an importative one. Therefore, it must be asked what difference it would make to our interpretation of life if there were a God distinct from the world. As the idea of God functions in the Semitic religions, perhaps its meaning could be at least partly formulated: the ideal of an ethical humanity will assuredly one day be realized. (The formulation of this difference is a main task of Jewish, Christian, and Islamic theology and demands great care and rigor of thought. Therefore this brief sentence should not be taken as exhausting by any means the possible importance of the idea of a God distinct from the world; it is given only as an example. But let us agree for the moment that something like this represents the importance of the statement.) Then one must inquire what range of facts could yield such a meaning; what metaphysical states of affairs would be incompatible with it, and what would be compatible; what, if any, would be required for it to hold.

The Christian tradition has held acceptable a number of quite divergent metaphysical conceptions of God; for example, Augustine's conception of God in terms of Platonic "being itself," in contrast with Pseudo-Dionysius' idea of God as beyond all being; Aquinas' concept of Pure Act, Tillich's idea of the Ground of Being, or Whitehead's

Valuation of the World. Any of these may be theologically legitimate for a Christian, but none can be binding on him, because it is not clear that any of them is entailed by the meaning which the Christian tradition assigns to God. Likewise the question of the relationship of God to the world cannot be settled, for a religious tradition, on metaphysical grounds. The point of departure must be the interpretation of life that it implies. Theological inquiry about the nature of God or his relation to the world is one concerning the range of metaphysical possibilities compatible with a particular vision of human life.

The width of the spectrum of facts considered able to give the desired meaning, or make a particular difference to people, cannot be settled once and for all beforehand by logical analysis of the meaning itself. If a friend tells me, for example, "I have a newfound confidence in myself," I know that an important difference has been made to him by something or other. But precisely what it was, or even what general class of experience he has had or discovery he has made, I cannot tell simply from this difference itself. One thing, no doubt, is immediately clear: whatever it was, it did not (unless he is hallucinating) stand in contradiction to this difference. For example, I would be reasonably certain that it was not because he had just been fired from his job that he had this new confidence in himself, or because his wife had left him (unless her character was such as to make that a matter for congratulation) or because he had just received an unusually large assessment of his income tax. Similarly with a religious tradition. There will necessarily be some possible states of affairs that would be incompatible with the meaning which forms the heart of the tradition, and others that though compatible do not provide the support they should.

The boundaries of the spectrum are set by contradiction. Candidates for the position of the original fact are ruled out if they necessarily yield a meaning which would contradict the meaning in question. But we cannot always be certain *a priori* what facts are compatible and what are incompatible with a meaning. The history of Christianity provides abundant examples of beliefs about matters of fact which were once thought to be in contradiction to the meaning of the religion, but were accepted by later generations as compatible with it. There was a time, not very long ago, when the generality of Christians rejected the theory of evolution, especially that of the "simian descent of man," as the plaque commemorating the Scopes trial puts it. They rejected it because they thought, among other things, that the effect of the theory would be to destroy the idea of creation, especially that of the human soul. The idea of creation appears to have the religious function (at least partly) of enhancing the authority of the God who judges, and so of reinforcing the certainty of justice to come. The issue is the Christian interpretation of life. But the thinking of Christians has ceased to consider evolution as a religious problem. The same sort of thing can be pointed out in such issues as the creation of the world in seven days, the sun standing still in the book of Joshua, which brought about the downfall of Galileo as well as of the Philistines, and the literary genera of the Bible, the doubtful character of the infancy narratives of Jesus, and so on. In these and many other cases the general body of the Christian church has come to consider acceptable candidates for the position of metaphysical or historical fact which it once held to be in contradiction to its faith.

This difficulty is not the peculiar property of Christianity. The philosophy presented in a majority of the Upanishads is an extreme form of idealism. All the different things we experience, including ourselves, are one with the Absolute, and thus with each other. The unity of all things in the One is their reality. Their individual differentiations are an illusion. A succession of these illusions, in reincarnation, must usually be passed through before unity with the One, the true Self, is achieved. The general thrust of the interpretation of life implied in this "nondualist" metaphysical system has already been outlined: man's chief problem in life is himself, more exactly, that part of him which suffers, the suffering self, his individual existence which lays him open to the painfulness and restrictions of plurality. The ideal solution proposed is the discovery of, and so unity with, the true, hidden Self which overcomes the painfulness of plurality. This discovery of one's true Self is possible, but not guaranteed; man possesses within himself the resources needed to achieve it. It would not necessarily be a contradiction of this to reject the vast metaphysical scaffolding of Hinduism, the doctrine that individuality is an illusion, or the accompanying notion of reincarnation. The Samkhya system acknowledges an ultimate plurality of selves, and Kumarila, of the Purva Mimamsa school, denies the very existence of a creator of the world, yet these are recognized as orthodox. Dualist and nondualist Hinduism stand in metaphysical contradiction to one another, yet both are considered orthodox.

Early Buddhism, though it claimed to eschew metaphysics, and is not commonly considered to rest as a religion on historical events in the sense that the Semitic religions do, still stems from the conviction that Gautama became the Buddha, that he attained enlightenment and Nirvana. Nirvana itself is described in what sometimes appear to be metaphysical terms. Much of the Buddhist world, both Theravada and Mahayana, retains from Brahmanism a notion, though vague, of reincarnation.

The interpretation of human life which characterized early Buddhism has been described in outline in the previous chapter. Life is suffering. We suffer because of our foolish desires. The remedy lies at hand—release, abandonment, the extinction of craving. That this is the meaning of Buddhism, in the sense in which we have been using the word "meaning," is clearly stated in the Buddha's Sermon at Benares. We scarcely have any other religion founded so explicitly and precisely on an interpretation of life rather than on a set of views about metaphysics or history.

Now when we consider how slight our critical historical knowledge of the Buddha is, for example, that the earliest texts of his speeches date from centuries after his death, is it necessary, in order to preserve this hope and even the confidence in these means to achieve it, to insist on the historical figure of the Buddha as one who achieved the perfection of enlightenment? It would not be a contradiction of the Buddha's vision of life if the doctrine of reincarnation or the belief in the historicity of Gautama were denied.

The Zen sect of Buddhism, taking its point of departure from devotional Mahayana and the search for union with the Buddha, proclaimed that he was to be found not in devotional practices, but within the heart of the seeker, and came around full circle to an emphasis on contemplation, especially the contemplation of nature; the person of the Buddha receded into the background altogether in Zen. But it is still quite possible to say that Zen Buddhism is Buddhism (though an adherent of Zen is equally capable, with typical perversity, of saying that it is not).

A classical doctrine of Islam is that the Koran was revealed verbally by God to Mohammed. Let us imagine, for the sake of argument, that one day it should be proved beyond all reasonable doubt that the Koran was written some years before the birth of Mohammed. Such a state of affairs would by no means stand in contradiction to the ethical, Pelagian interpretation of life which characterizes Islam as a religion. Islam as a religion would scarcely collapse in such an event. The millions of human beings whose lives are formed and fashioned by it will not on that account abandon Islam.

It was also part of early Muslim orthodoxy that the Koran had existed in heaven from all eternity before it was revealed. Yet the Shiite sects have not accepted this and are not on that count denied the full status of Muslims by their fellows. The mystical philosophy of the Sufis was first hailed as a heresy and persecuted. Subsequently it was adopted into Ghazzali's classic synthesis of Muslim theology.

The argument of this chapter so far has been that it is not possible to determine *a priori* and beforehand once and for all where the boundaries of the spectrum fall, because we cannot tell *a priori* precisely and completely what facts will contradict the meaning of a religion.

As people's understanding of the world they live in grows, and their horizons widen, sometimes against their will, their comprehension of their religious tradition may well deepen, they come to appreciate a little more adequately the historical processes by which it has developed, and they become more occupied with its point, with what it is driving at, than with the garments in which it has decked itself in the course of time.

The spectrum of possible facts which will be considered compatible with a religion and capable of making the difference to man of which it speaks will vary according to all these factors and others. It will vary from person to person, and as far as a religious community is concerned, from age to age, as one understanding of the world, and of what can be reasonably believed, is replaced by another. Attempts to formulate statements of fact on the basis of a religious tradition can never be final. The present community will be replaced by another generation which understands the world differently, and present efforts to discover how it really was or is may be judged successful to the extent that they will have enabled themselves to be fruitfully surpassed.

Any factitive statement in religion stands for the whole spectrum of possibilities which could yield the meaning of that religion. The fact has a representative character, and any other possibility within the spectrum can take its place. The statement that Moses received a revelation on Mt. Sinai is supported by the Old Testament, but so is the statement that he received it on Mt. Horeb. Both yield the same religious meaning for Judaism and Christianity. The utterance of one deputizes for the other. A Christian may say that Jesus rose from the dead with a body which belongs to our customary space and time. Karl Rahner has suggested as an alternative, which should be quite acceptable to Christians, that he arose from the dead with a body which does not belong to our space and time. Each of these is a laudable attempt to say something useful. But both conceptions fulfill the requirements of the Christian tradition and either one, when it is made, stands for and represents the entire spectrum of original possibilities. It is a *locum tenens*, and any other one within the spectrum may some day be considered more likely to yield the meaning and therefore closer to the original fact.

This interpretation of the way factitive statements in religion are to be taken is not uttered as a critique from a standpoint outside religion, but holds on religion's own terms and on the terms of any particular religion. A psychologist may assure us that factitive religious beliefs are the product of psychic tensions, and should therefore be regarded as illusions. An anthropologist may inform us that they are an instrument of social control, and the question of their truth-value scarcely arises. Such judgments are made from a position external to the enterprise of religion; their merit depends on the solidity of their basis within their own disciplines. But in addition to such appraisals from outside, completeness and even fairness require that we have available an assessment that takes into account the standpoint of the religious person himself and the history of religious traditions on their own terms. Here, as elsewhere, contentment with externality involves a risk of being like Caesar's augurer, who opened the entrails of the beast but did not find its heart.

One remarkable feature of factitive religious language mentioned earlier has not been dealt with further. There are very few occasions where people make unconditional assertions about the future. One of them, and apparently the chief one, is in matters of religious belief. A significant proportion of factitive religious assertions are made in the future tense, especially in the religions of Semitic origin. It is stated that God will judge the living and the dead, that there will be a resurrection of the body, that there will be a heaven and a hell. It is possible for a conditional assertion in the future tense to be true or false now. If I had cold sardines for supper tonight, then tomorrow it will be the case that I had cold sardines for supper, so I can say that it is true now that tomorrow I will have had cold sardines for supper. But an *unconditional*, or categorical, assertion in the future tense cannot be either true or false *now*. "He will come tomorrow" uttered without any conditions attached is neither true nor untrue at the time when it is spoken. The notions of truth or falsity do not apply to it at this moment. Mankind seems to possess a sense that this is so, and as a result practically never indulges in unconditional future assertions. All our ordinary assertions about the future are found on investigation to be wisely conditional, insofar as they state some fact. Normally if I say "He will come tomorrow," I understand that he will come if he can, if there is not some accident to prevent him; or perhaps I mean only that he intends to come tomorrow.

In religions, however, this conditionality is sometimes thrown aside. Certain knowledge of future events is claimed. It is clear that such statements serve some function, have some purpose, and therefore cannot be dismissed as meaningless. But it is not their function, even as factitive statements, to state a truth. We are left with a question here that is quite fascinating and which still awaits an answer, namely, "What is their function, specifically as assertions about the future, now?

NOTE

1. The proposal that in religion we begin with an interpretation of life (a "seeing-as," or a perspective) and conclude from that to the facts (metaphysical or historical) rather than vice-versa, as commonly assumed, is in general a natural derivative from a Kantian or critical realism, which acknowledges the subjectively conditioned quality of our perception, and sees this as our only access to the facts, but holds that it does indeed give us access to the world of fact, and is not merely a distortion that shuts reality off from us. Such critical realism is represented in the work of Dilthey, and has been especially developed by one branch of scholars in the sociology of knowledge—Max Scheler, *Die Wissensformen und die Gesellschaft*; Karl Mannheim, *Ideology and Utopia*; Werner Stark, *The Sociology of Knowledge*; and Thomas Luckman and Peter Berger, *The Social Construction of Reality*.

If it is once agreed that a primary function of religious language is to present a way of interpreting life, as Wisdom has suggested, it is no large step to conclude that in religion *a fortiori* we do not begin with hard fact and conclude to an interpretation of it, but rather we begin with an interpretation, a way of looking at life and experience, and if we wish to get closer to hard fact, it must be through the avenue of interpretation.

2 a.) The problem of the significance of factitive statements for religion first presented itself to the West as the problem of what to do with the literal sense of the myths of Mediterranean religion. The initial resolution of this problem by men desirous of retaining the myth was allegorical interpretation. Stoic and neo-Platonic writers, such as Cornutus and Plutarch, tell what the stories of Hephaistos or of Isis and Osiris *really* mean—they turn out to mean Stoic or neo-Platonic philosophy. The Stoic and neo-Platonic writers abandon the literal sense of the myths in favor of an allegorical sense. The early Christian writers, however, faced with the same problem, could not so easily abandon the literal sense of the stories they were interpreting. Clement, Origen, and the other Alexandrian Christian writers then keep the literal sense of the Christian stories, which in this case is factitive, and add the allegorical sense as a "higher" or more "spiritual" one, though clearly it is often the more important sense in their eyes.

The creedal conflicts of the fourth and fifth centuries, and the subsequent view that religion (= true religion = Christianity) could be defined in terms of faith plus morals, of belief and conduct, laid emphasis on the literal sense of factitive statements. One result of this was the development of a sophisticated metaphysics in the service of religion, which reached its high-water mark in medieval scholasticism. The facts were explained by an appropriate metaphysics and in this way were defused or submerged as a problem.

The reemergence of the problem, of how to take factitive statements in religion and what status or significance to assign to them, was occasioned by the rise of Pietism in Germany at the close of the seventeenth century. For the medieval view that religion (Christianity) consisted in faith and morals, Pietism substituted the conviction that the essence of true religion lies in a spiritual rebirth of the individual which is an object of inner experience or feeling. Religion thus became centrally religious feeling, religious experience.

Systematic form was given to the pietist view by Schleiermacher's definition of religion as a feeling of absolute dependence (Gefühl der schlechtinnigen Abhängigkeit, *The Christian Faith*, intro. Ch. 1). It follows from this that the primary function of religious assertions can be neither cognitive nor ethical.

> "Wherefore, my friends, belief must be something different
> from a mixture of opinions about God and the world, and
> of precepts for one life or two. Piety cannot be an instinct
> craving for a mess of metaphysical and ethical crumbs."
> (*On Religion*, Ch. 2.)

> "I consider it very wrong that out of things so disparate as
> modes of knowing and modes of acting, you patch together
> an untenable something, and call it religion."
> (Ibid.)

Granted that the primary or characteristic function of religious language is not factitive, a question still remains about
the status of fact-statements for religion in Schleiermacher's
view. In the *Speeches on Religion* he writes, "Had I not pre-
supposed God and immortality I could not have said what I
said." They are not the principal things in religion, but they are
necessary presuppositions for it. In his later work, *The Christian
Faith*, however, he writes that "the term 'God' . . . is nothing
more than the expression of the feeling of absolute dependence";
and already in the *Speeches* the only immortality that is of
significance for religion is that "which we can have in this tem-
poral life." "In the midst of finitude to be one with the Infinite,
and in every moment to be eternal is the immortality of religion"
(*Speeches*, II.) It seems very doubtful whether in the last analysis statements functioning as factitive could have any real bearing on Schleiermacher's religion. A similar position was ascribed
within the Roman Catholic Church to those whom Pius X la-
beled "Modernists" in his encyclical letter *Pascendi* (1907).
These persons are alleged to have attributed to religious beliefs a
purely subjective sense, designed to fulfill a religious need. Pre-
sumably factitive statements would be religiously entirely irrelevant for a "modernist."

The problem of the religious significance of metaphysical or
historical facts has been dealt with most explicitly in recent
times by writers espousing an extreme existential interpretation
of Christianity. For Karl Barth, at least in his earlier writings,
Aristotle's Prime Mover is not merely irrelevant, but positively
unchristian, on the grounds that it is religious, Christianity being
not a religion which is the work of corrupt man but revelation,
the word of God.

Rudolf Bultmann, who has probably done more than any other to make the historical question painful for Christians, seems to be selective in the matter of the bearing of factitive statements in general on Christianity. Christianity can get along without a factually historical Jesus, but not without a God who acts in history (cf., e.g., *Jesus Christ and Mythology*).

2 b.) The position I am defending here, that importative statements require at least a *spectrum of facts* to back them up, is directed against the extremes of existential interpretation, as being epistemologically unsatisfactory. This position was at least adumbrated by the nineteenth century American theologian Horace Bushnell. Bushnell developed a detailed theory of language and was also unwilling to dispense entirely with any factitive element for religion. His solution is to ascribe to factitive statements, e.g., creedal formulas, a certain elasticity of function.

> "Considering the infirmities of language, therefore, all formulas of doctrine should be held in a certain spirit of accommodation. They cannot be pressed to the letter, for the very sufficient reason that the letter is never true. They can be regarded only as proximate representations." ("Preliminary Dissertation on Language," in *God in Christ*, Hartford, 1849, p. 81.)

> "Language is rather an instrument of suggestion, than of absolute conveyance for thought." (Ibid., p. 88.)

3. Tense logic has received attention from logicians only recently, and little work has been done on the logic of unconditional future statements that adds anything to Aristotle. To those interested in pursuing this topic, Arthur Prior's book *Past, Present and Future* (Oxford, 1967) is recommended, especially the final sections, and also "The Formalities of Omniscience" in the same author's *Papers on Time and Tense* (Oxford, 1968).

3. Purpose

"Why do you love truth?"
"For truth's sake."
"Why do you love justice?"
"For the sake of justice!"
"Why do you love goodness?"
"For goodness' sake."
"And why do you live?"
"On my honor, I don't know—I like
to live!"

— Meister Eckhardt

An assertion of meaning is an assertion of a special sort of
intelligibility. To claim that a thing has meaning is to
claim at least that in some way it makes sense, that it is
capable of being understood. Intelligibility in turn is a
matter of order; understanding is the perception of order.
The sort of order that constitutes meaning is not a mere
arrangement of parts, a pattern, a static set of relationships,
however; there is a special satisfaction to the mind in the
perception of that sort of order which is directedness towards a goal, and it is this kind of order that confers meaning. There is an important sense in which we understand a
thing by perceiving its purpose. This can happen in two
very distinct ways: we can perceive the purpose for which it
already exists, the purpose inherent in it, or we can see how
we can use it to achieve some end. There is a great difference between these two. In the one case the thing already
has meaning; in the other we bestow meaning on it. In
either case it becomes intelligible.

A farmer digging a field turns up an oddly shaped piece
of stone. He does not see what, if anything, it was fashioned
to do; he does not see that he could make any use of it
himself; it is not intelligible to him, "has no meaning" for

him, he throws it away and goes on working. His wife, however, had she seen it, might have exclaimed, "Aha! That's just what I need to pound the meat with!" or "That would make an elegant doorstop." It has become intelligible to her, "has meaning" for her. An archaeologist coming across it might have said, "This is clearly a large axhead of the type used by Mousterian man for maintaining domestic tranquility." It has then become intelligible to him too, has meaning for him, though in a quite different way. In each case the intelligibility, the meaning, has come from a perception of purpose, one extrinsic, of a purpose that the thing could be put to, the other intrinsic, of the purpose for which it was initially fashioned.

Intelligibility can be desired for its own sake; that is curiosity. But it is also our chief means of achieving control. Inability to understand a situation renders us helpless in it. Our security is threatened when we do not understand what is going on. Growth in understanding is in general the chief promoter of our safety and our confidence. The same is true of the intelligibility of our own personal existence. Although understanding by no means guarantees control, it is a first indispensable step towards it. The intelligiblity and so the meaning of our lives is therefore not only a matter of curiosity, it is of the utmost importance to us.

The principal frustrator of meaning is absurdity. A thing is absurd not when it is not understood, but when it appears to be not capable of being understood, when it is experienced, in itself and not because of any intellectual inadequacy in the person experiencing it, as unintelligible. Absurdity is intrinsic unintelligibility. That is, it is not mere lack of purpose, but intrinsic inability to contain purpose. To assert that a thing is absurd is to assert both that it is not of itself already directed towards any goal, and that it is not capable of being directed towards any goal, of being used to achieve an end; and also, of course, that it is not capable of constituting a goal itself. Sometime or other we have probably all given our head a good bang on the roof on entering a car. A fair part of the frustration this occasions comes from the pointlessness of the thing. For a few moments I am unable, despite the utmost piety, to attribute any purpose to the torture. It is absurd, and I suffer from the absurdity as much as from the dent in my skull.

The absurd is functionless. It does not simply happen to lack a function at the moment, but appears incapable of possessing any function. A thing which is seen to be capable of possessing a function is by that fact intelligible and has meaning. In this sense meaning and functionality are interchangeable terms. To speak of meaning is to speak of a function either already possessed or capable of being bestowed.

Many people come early in life to an experience which suggests not only its own absurdity, but that of life as a whole. A situation where no matter what I do it will be wrong, a sudden illness at just the time when I needed to be well and alert, the shock of meeting a strange viciousness, an apparently undeserved hostility in other people, the failure of a friendship, the slow, agonizing death of someone close to me, the prospect of my own death, once it comes home to me that not only other people but I myself will one day cease to exist: these experiences present themselves to us as instances of purposelessness, of functionlessness, of unintelligibility, and of intrinsic unintelligibility. As isolated events they can be extremely powerful. Taken together they easily build up into a massive suggestion that human life as a whole is absurd: if it were not, such things would not happen.

No matter how strongly these experiences may suggest

absurdity, however, it would not be accurate to say that in themselves they constitute experiences of absurdity. There is no experience which is not interpreted, and an interpretation may color experience itself so effectively as to prevent a person from even entertaining the notion that what is being encountered is really absurd. St. Paul's statement "For those who love God all things work together unto good," expresses an overriding interpretation of life which transfigures particular experiences. The most we can say is that an experience or set of experiences may suggest absurdity, and may suggest it more strongly or less. Part of the significance of interpretations of life lies precisely in their ability to transform experience, to predetermine the range of forms that it can take, so that a suggestion in the opposite direction is overcome.

Faced with experiences suggestive of absurdity on a massive scale, how shall we react? When the suggestion becomes sufficiently comprehensive or total, the continuance of the human enterprise is at stake. We are threatened with futility, with inward defeat. How is it possible to hope?

There are a number of ways in which we can respond to such experience. Every organism possesses, so long as it is operating properly, a physical vitality, a drive which pushes it on to preserve itself, and makes it determined not to yield itself up. This vital force naturally leads to a sort of animal optimism, a "kind of organic attachment to myself which makes me imagine final liberation in the midst of danger even where the future seems most threatening," as Gabriel Marcel puts it. In this sense can we do anything else but hope? But this force survives only so long as the organism is healthy. If the vital powers decay, physically through illness or emotionally and mentally through the onset of some severe shock, this natural optimism fades and slackens, just at the time when an inner dynamism is most needed. This organic vitality is not to be mistaken for hope.

Another force which gives energy to counteract the negative and diminishing experiences of life consists in counterbalancing positive experiences, of friendship, love, and encouragement, of success in overcoming obstacles. The experience of success is indispensable for the healthy psychological development of the person. What these positive experiences achieve is a psychological vitality, an extension and strengthening of organic vitality. They create the psychological possibility of hope, but not hope itself. They operate largely in the realm of the unconscious; but the conscious question which they assume still needs an answer, whether I really am of value in the scheme of things. Perhaps the love shown me is in fact futile, and the world and my existence is absurd. This question is answered only by the conscious intellectual vision which constitutes an interpretation of life.

Our experience of life taken as a whole is ambivalent. There are individual experiences suggestive of absurdity, which can accumulate into a large suggestion of general absurdity. There are also individual experiences rich with the suggestion of order, intelligibility, and purpose, which can accumulate into a large suggestion of comprehensive intelligibility. Experience itself does not settle the issue. Its ambivalence is removed, and unity of vision achieved, by a decision to interpret life in a particular way. Two elements stand out here: the mind's coherent act of interpretation unifies and overcomes the ambivalence of experience; this cannot be achieved in any other way—though a person may have little reflective awareness of precisely what he is doing. And such an interpretation must in the end be a decision rather than a logical deduction: I decide to interpret life this way rather than that. Although reasoning may play a lengthy and even painful role, there is no way in which it can of itself bridge the ambiguity of experience, which must serve as the final criterion.

The reasons for which such a decision is in fact made may be manifold, perhaps purely emotional or biochemical. They do not affect the truth or accuracy or adequacy of the interpretation. That would be as if a man were maintaining that the angles inside a triangle add up to two right angles, and someone objected: "You say that because you are a bourgeois intellectual." The question of how such a decision is best made, how an interpretation of life may be justified or invalidated, will be dealt with in a subsequent chapter.

There are three alternative answers which an interpretation of life may give to the question of the relationship between life and meaning or purpose. One is that human existence is indeed absurd, intrinsically unintelligible, incapable of containing purpose. A second alternative is that human life, while not intrinsically unintelligible, not incapable of containing purpose, does not in fact bear any purpose within itself, is not of itself directed towards any goal, but is capable of having purpose bestowed on it by the individual, and so can become intelligible extrinsically, by a person's own action. The third alternative is that human existence is already in itself directed towards some goal, contains purpose within itself, and so is intrinsically intelligible independently of the insight or action of the individual. In the third case life has meaning; in the second case it does not have meaning of itself, but it can receive it, and in the first case it is incapable of being meaningful.

The relation seen between life and purpose varies according to the different elements that go to make up the interpretation of life. If it can be considered, for working purposes, to consist of the three elements mentioned earlier, (1) a proposal as to what constitutes man's principal problem in life, (2) a proposal of an ideal state of affairs which would remedy that problem, and (3) a proposal about the realization of that remedy, each of these factors plays a distinctive role, the first two giving the form of the purpose envisaged, and the third its actuality or absence.

The first element, the principal problem, specifies the form in which the threat of absurdity is experienced most intensely. The rest of the interpretation is based on this.

The second element, the ideal solution, specifies the purpose itself, the particular form which overcomes the threat of absurdity, and is to be set up as the goal of human endeavor. Because it specifies the purpose of life, the second element has a role of quite special importance in determining the shape and character of the life-interpretation. It also, by the nature of the case, determines in advance the value system which will dominate the way of life deriving from the interpretation.

But it is the third element, the proposal about the realization of the ideal, which determines the possibility and actuality of purposefulness and intelligibility in human life. It also, as a corollary, decides the metaphysical system needed to support the interpretation, and the temperature at which the vision will operate.

Realization of the ideal solution may be considered in every sense impossible; in that case human existence is absurd. Outstanding examples of this conviction can be found in contemporary literature.

Realization of the ideal may be considered possible, but not certain. In this case there is no conviction that the world is intrinsically purposeful or intelligible, but there is a conviction that human life can have purpose and intelligibility bestowed on it. This view is characteristic of the

religions indigenous to China and India, the religions clas-
sified as "primitive" of Africa and Australia, and the ar-
chaic religions of the Greeks, Romans, and most Indo-
Europeans. In this century it has been very well expressed
in the writings of Dr. D. T. Suzuki on Zen. This view
has been so widely spread, and so consistently held, that in
the history of religions it must be accorded the status of the
common or ordinary opinion.

In third place, realization of the ideal may be expected
with certainty. In this case human life has a goal and purpose built into it, it is intrinsically intelligible and meaningful. This view is characteristic of the ethical religions:
those of Semitic origin, Zoroastrianism, and Marxism: all of
these look forward to a public state of salvation that is
certain to come, although the private participation of any
given individual in it is not guaranteed. If it is pointed out
that the notion of an "eschaton" is, relatively speaking,
something of a newcomer on the stage, and after a period of
popularity is again felt by many to be somewhat extraordinary, that should not be taken as a value judgment against
it, but merely as an observation of fact. The question, what
is man for? which seems to the westerner so obvious and
urgent, is a novel one, and to a large portion of mankind
does not seem to have been a matter of concern.

To sum up the reflections of this chapter so far: the notion of "the meaning of life" is a factor of the directedness
of life towards some final goal, it is a matter of overall
purpose, and so of hope. It depends directly on the degree
of certainty with which realization is expected of what is
held to be the ideal solution for man's principal problem.

It is a matter of history that such a certainty has been
asserted only by those religions which are characterized by a
predominantly ethical concern, and which depend upon
highly developed notions of guilt, sin, conscience, and

therefore judgment; and by philosophies or parareligions, such as the Marxist, which are derivative of the ethical religions. The notion of an eschaton implies that there has been a transition from "justice must be done" to "justice will be done." If the idea is to be maintained that life has a meaning, then the certainty must be upheld of a future event that will remedy man's wrongs. If this certainty regarding the future is abandoned, there is no possibility of retaining the idea that life has a meaning, except insofar as we bestow one on it, which is a very different thing. However, it has become increasingly difficult, in a world where scientific method has once prevailed, to look forward to any future event with certainty. Aristotle already saw that logically a statement about the future is neither true nor false at the time it is uttered, as noted above.

It is consistent with this development that the question eventually ceases to be of interest, whether life possesses a meaning of itself. For most of the time, most people are sustained in the sense that their life has a meaning by the smaller day-to-day purposes they work for, by the functions they experience themselves to be fulfilling. It is only when these outer bastions are broken, when illness, age, or youth, deprive one of the experience of being useful, of performing some function, that the notion of an intrinsic purpose and meaning to life becomes particularly useful; it is a conviction for times of crisis. If it has in the meantime become impossible or untenable, there remains the other alternative, of an overriding purpose which we ourselves bestow on life. This has in any event been the usual solution of mankind; it has been systematically developed in religions such as Hinduism and Buddhism or Jainism, and it is well exemplified in some current forms of mysticism.

Two other factors are dictated by the degree of certainty with which the ideal remedy for man's ills is expected to be realized. One is the necessity of postulating a system of "facts," whether metaphysical or historical, to support an interpretation of life.

If the realization is considered impossible, then since human existence is absurd, there is no need to postulate any metaphysical system, any underlying structure to the universe. On the contrary, the postulate of a metaphysical structure in the universe would undermine the life-interpretation, which rests on a denial of intelligible structure.

If realization of the ideal is possible but not certain, a metaphysical system may be very useful, but it is not necessary and can be done without. These two alternatives are represented by the Upanishads and the Vedanta system of Hinduism, as well as by Jain philosophy and by early Buddhism. By adopting the thought of the Vedanta the Hindu tradition explicitly based itself on a metaphysical system; the function of the Vedantist assertion of the oneness of all things is to maintain the positive possibility of the overcoming of conflict and suffering, though it does not render that victory in any way assured. The Buddha saw that the same goal could be attained without metaphysical speculation.

> "The religious life . . . does not depend on the dogma that the world is eternal, nor . . . on the dogma that the world is not eternal. Whether . . . the world is eternal or not eternal, there still remains birth, old age, death, sorrow, lamentation, misery, grief, and despair, for the extinction of which in the present life I am prescribing." (Majjhima-Nikaya, Sutta 63, tr. H. C. Warren)

But by contrast, if it is proposed that human life has a goal and purpose built into it, a metaphysical system must of necessity be postulated which will account for this. The assertion that a definite event, such as a universal judgment, can be relied upon unconditionally to take place at some time in the future is an extraordinary one. It cannot be arrived at by experience. This certainty about the future demands an explanation, or it collapses. In the Semitic religions the idea of a personal God fulfills this function; if the good are to be rewarded and the wicked punished, there must be someone who will do this, and he must possess the qualities needed to carry out the task: holiness, power, love, knowledge. In Hegelian and Marxist philosophy a similar function is fulfilled by "Mind" and the "world-historical process." If mankind is destined to achieve a state of ultimate freedom, or a classless society, there must be some force at work in the world which will ensure that this comes about, though to this end it need not necessarily be personal. It will perhaps prove to be the most serious weakness of Marxism that it has not given enough attention to its metaphysical underpinnings and to their credibility. At the present time all systems of thought that have looked forward with assurance to some future ideal state of affairs, the Semitic religions, Marxism, and also the liberal tradition, are having their self-confidence undermined by the growth and spread of a scientific method and mentality which has proven its effectiveness within its own limits, and which appears to make any such knowledge and confidence impossible.

A difference of metaphysical structure will also be required by the other elements in the notion of the realization of the ideal, that of the location of the resources for it. If the interpretation of life is Pelagian, that it is up to man to save himself, the emphasis is likely to be on the immanence of God in the world, his unity with it, and perhaps identity with it, so far as God can be known at all. Mysticism is characteristically Pelagian. The unity with the world of God as known is also a logically consistent position for a Muslim. If the interpretation of life is saviorist, that man cannot save himself, then the emphasis will logically be on the distinction of God from the world, his trans-cedence, as in Christianity. These notions function logically as metaphysical postulates required as explanations to support a particular conviction about the place of purpose in human life, and especially about the assurance of its attainment.

Another matter governed by the degree of certainty with which the realization of the ideal state of things is expected is the temperature of the religion. By this I mean the level of intensity at which it tends to operate, its inherent energy as a system, often shown by its uncompromisingness. Different visions function naturally at different temperatures. The extremes are stoicism and fanaticism. If it is believed that realization of the ideal is impossible, the vision of life must of necessity be sober, *nüchtern*, though of course the conviction itself, like most others, may be held with passion. If it is believed that realization of the ideal is possible but not certain, then the vision possesses a higher level of intensity, but will still be relatively cool, or only moderately warm. The Confucian tradition is the classic example of religion operating at a moderate, but persistent, temperature.

By contrast, if it is believed that realization of the ideal is certain to be achieved, if a Kingdom of God or a classless society is bound to come, then the vision operates at a high temperature, at a level of great intensity, with increasing intolerance and unwillingness to compromise. It is perhaps capable of calling forth a more emotional commitment from its followers. I am not speaking here about the temperament of individuals, but the inherent energy of a vision. It may well be that the temperament of a people is fanatical and that for that very reason they need a religion that is cool and moderate.

The aim of this chapter has been to point out the implications of an interpretation of life for the question of "the meaning of life." Meaning in this context is a form of intelligibility given only with the perception or creation of purpose. The relationship of purpose to human life as a whole, whether the idea is considered quite inapplicable, or capable of being bestowed, or inherent and intrinsic, is decided by the degree of certainty with which the realization of the ideal is looked forward to. The torment of Gilgamesh, the threat of absurdity, is overcome only by a vision of purpose.

It is a characteristic of religious visions of life that they assert purpose, in either the one way or the other, for human life as a whole. By this they inspire a radical hope, which is capable of vast energy, as history witnesses. It seems doubtful whether the same effect is ever achieved by other means.

Not every interpretation of life supports hope; but it is a feature of religious interpretations of life that they do. A religion is the expression of a desire to hope, given form by the experience of a concrete threat to hope. The result is a way of looking at the experience so that it ceases to be a threat: it is interpreted. The interpretation in its turn may demand unseen facts to back it up. There is great danger here of wishful thinking; in the end any belief that supports hope may do. If the continuance of the human enterprise depends on our being able to have hope, then a case can perhaps be made that indeed in a crisis any belief that supports hope will do, at least for a while until the crisis is past. It has been suggested often enough however that the continuance of the human enterprise does not depend on our being able to hope, that in fact we may be better off without it. The persistence of this disagreement confirms what was observed above, that experience alone does not decide the issue. Our experience of life has already been colored by our interpretation of it.

NOTE

The word "meaning" is used in many different senses. It seems that these can be embraced under three headings: (1) meaning as the indication by one thing of another thing, (2) meaning as importance, (3) meaning as intention or purpose.

1. The use of the term "meaning" in the first sense occurs in two main subsenses:

a) the indication by one thing of another in virtue of an intrinsic connection, or one in the nature of things. We use the word in this sense when we say that a falling barometer means rain; more government spending means an increase in taxes; her shyness really means that she loves him. A means B here in the sense that there is an association between the two in virtue of which A is a natural sign of B.

b) the indication by one thing of another in virtue of an artificial, man-made or socially conventional connection. This is the sense in which we speak of symbols meaning something, as that the red light at the intersection means traffic must stop. It is also the sense in which we speak of words or sentences having meaning.

A distinction is commonly made, following Gottlob Frege, in regard to the meaning of language, between "sense" and "reference." The two phrases "morning star" and "evening star" have the same reference—they both refer to the planet Venus. But they have different senses because they employ different characterizations. Similarly "featherless biped" and "mammal endowed with the power of speech" have the same reference, namely, every human being, but different senses. The reference is said to constitute the "extension" of the term, i.e., the class of all those things the term applies to. The sense is said to constitute the term's "intension," i.e., the characteristics it identifies. Either sense or reference can constitute the meaning of a term. This aspect of meaning receives most attention in contemporary philosophy and linguistics.

2. The word "meaning" is used to indicate importance, in statements such as "travel used to mean a lot to me once, but now I'm too old, and comfort is more important to me," or "my relationship with him means a great deal to me." (It is in this sense that the word was used in Chapter 1.)

3. A common use of "meaning," and especially of the verb form "to mean," is to indicate purpose or intention. If someone remarks "I do sometimes use nasty words, but I don't mean to," or "the injury was not meant," we take this as a declaration about deliberate intention, or purpose. "Say, for what were hop-yards meant, or why was Burton built on Trent" (A. E. Houseman). "He means well by you."

In the noun form we use "meaning" in the sense of purpose or intention when we ask about someone's strange activity: What is the meaning of this odd behavior? We are asking, what is he up to, what is his aim?

We speak of the "meaning" of a law in the sense of its spirit, or intent, in contrast to its letter. Similarly, if I am trying to express myself, but doing a bad job of it, I may say: If you get my meaning, that is, if you see what I intend to say, rather than the words I have actually used.

It would be misguided to assume *a priori* that this variety of senses can or should be brought under one common denominator. However, they do have certain elements in common. The most outstanding feature which all these senses of "meaning" have is intentionality, in Husserl's sense. An act is intentional in this sense, not in that it has a purpose, but that it is directed towards an object. Consciousness, for example, must always be consciousness *of something*. Similarly, to mean is always to mean *something*. An indication of this is the fact that "to mean" is always a transitive verb. I can never say of something simply: "This means." Meaning is not a feature which rests in its subject, rather it points to something else beyond. Even if I wish to use meaning in the sense of importance or value, I cannot say: This means to me; but must give the verb an object: This means a lot, or a great deal to me.

When we ask the question, what is the meaning of life? what are we asking? Ninian Smart has suggested that this should be understood as a question about the value of life, rather than about its purpose (*The Philosophy of Religion*, Ch. 3.) We can have purposes, he remarks, that seem to have lost their meaning, as when I board the train to go to work, but my work does not mean much to me anymore. Furthermore, whenever we find that a thing has lost meaning for us, it is because it has lost value for us. Meaninglessness then consists in the absence of value. The point of Smart's view is that the concept would properly occur within any religion. In the view I am proposing, the notion "the meaning of life" is one that would properly occur only within the ethical religions, or those that see human life as intrinsically directed towards an eventual culmination, such as a judgment, or a resurrection.

Smart's case against purpose is weak: (a) to the extent that my work no longer has meaning for me I can equally well say that it no longer serves any purpose for me. (b) since meaning is clearly one kind of value, the absence of value will always imply absence of meaning. But that does not prevent meaning from being purpose. It simply implies that absence of value will always include absence of purpose, i.e., to the extent that a thing lacks value for me I cannot make it a purpose of mine.

Rather than get lost in an argument about words, it seems there might be more point to investigating the various ways in which different kinds of religion relate to both purpose and value.

The position taken here is closely related to that of the historian of Greek religion, Martin P. Nilsson, in his essay *Religion as Man's Protest Against the Meaninglessness of Events* (Lund, 1954): "The value which religion maintains is that life and events have a meaning, and if they are or seem to be meaningless, religion protests against the meaninglessness and tries to find a meaning in them, viz., to interpret them as having meaning." This Nilsson calls a "positive protest," and recognizes in addition a "negative protest," when "the meaninglessness of life and events is acknowledged, and man seeks his salvation in being freed, released from them."

4. Community

"Why are you killing me for your own
benefit? I am unarmed."
"Why, do you not live on the other
side of the water? My friend, if you
lived on this side, I should be a
murderer, but since you live on the
other side, I am a brave man and
it is right."

— Pascal

A community of persons is characterized by two things especially: what it allows shall count as knowledge, and what
it strives to attain as purpose. The principal function of a
religious community is to serve as a community of the most
important knowledge and of final purpose.

Knowledge is socially determined to a degree that largely
goes unrecognized. In some tribes of Australian aborigines a
medicine man is made in the following way: he is killed, his
internal organs are removed and replaced by special stones,
and he is then brought back to life. The details of this
event vary from tribe to tribe, but the general pattern is
common; there is a group of human beings where this *sort*
of thing constitutes knowledge. In the community of bio-
chemists, by contrast, such assertions do not at present pass
for knowledge. This is an extreme but simple instance of
the fact that what counts as knowledge varies from community to community.

Such radical divergence holds not only between groups
which belong to the past and those which belong to the
present. It also holds between groups of people who live
intimately side by side. Left wing political groups in the
United States know that the established economic and polit-

ical system is corrupt and destructive; right wing groups know that it is one of the country's chief glories.

Such communities, though closely contiguous, are mutually exclusive. However, the principle prevails equally among societies whose membership overlaps. Thus the sort of thing that counts as knowledge for the legal community, for instance, as evidence in a court of law, largely does not count as evidence in the scientific community; and the sort of thing that constitutes knowledge for the social sciences does not agree with what is allowed as knowledge by the physical sciences. Many kinds of things that count as knowledge within the intimacy of the family are not allowed to count as knowledge in a court of law or a laboratory.

Each individual is a member of numerous knowledge-communities, and as he moves from one to the other in the course of the day, as he steps out of his laboratory onto the street, buys a newspaper, runs his car into someone else's, and eventually arrives home to his family, the criteria change, and even perhaps conflict, for what counts as knowledge.

Although there may be striking differences of standards among the various knowledge-communities that a person is a member of, there is a tendency for them to harmonize with one another, rather than to conflict, so that a cultural unity emerges. Within a unified culture there will of course be conflicting convictions as to what specifically is true or false, but there will be general agreement as to the *kinds* of things that may be allowed as knowledge in different spheres. Without such generic agreement it would scarcely be possible to speak of "a culture." It is only in this general agreement that a culture as such exists.

A religion is a knowledge-community; it is characterized by an agreement that certain things shall be held as convictions. It is distinguished from other kinds of knowledge-communities in that its convictions express (what is considered to be) the most important knowledge.

The specific function which a religion fulfills as a community lies first in that it establishes as knowledge what would otherwise be a private conviction, and so sustains it in certainty. The fact that an individual arrives at a conviction does not yet confer on it the status of knowledge, outside certain apparently privileged realms of direct sense experience and of inner awareness, e.g., of one's own emotions. In general a private conviction becomes knowledge when it is accepted as such by a group. A Persian of the thirteenth century may have been convinced that democracy was the most desirable form of government, but that conviction would not then have counted as knowledge. Today it does possess the status of knowledge. Likewise an individual may arrive at a particular interpretation of life, for example, the Buddha's "Life is suffering." If he is surrounded exclusively by people who see things differently, his vision is seriously threatened and is not likely to endure long. But if his vision is shared by a group of people it acquires a special, quasi-objective certitude which cannot be obtained in any other way. Eventually, when the group attains sufficient size, or if its members talk only to one another, it will become an assumption, taken for granted and not questioned.

It is only in community that an interpretation of life attains the certainty which it needs to have if it is to function effectively for the individual.

A community is a number of people linked by some public bond. The bond may be of various kinds, but it can never be purely private and internal; ten people, scattered and unknown to one another, who think alike on some issue, do not constitute a community. They must first make contact with one another and discover their agreement. Every community must be at least partly physical, united by some physical and therefore public bonds, even if they are such things as words.

This implies that a person is likely to continue to share the outlook of a group only so long as he maintains some sort of physical contact with them. This will be especially true where the point of view being maintained in the community is one which applies more obviously to times of crisis than to ordinary everyday living. Conversely, if his contact with the group diminishes or disappears, it is extremely unlikely that he will continue to participate in their common outlook. What had previously been knowledge for him will gradually be replaced by other convictions.

This social character of knowledge, its dependence not only on the object of knowledge, but on the community of knowledge, is not only a psychological or a sociological fact, it is an epistemological one, inherent in the nature of human knowledge by reason of the social nature of the knowing subject. Knowledge has a social *a priori*, which both makes it possible in the first place, and also limits its scope.

Certainty is dependent on community; the group decides what shall count as knowledge. Conversely, it is the common fund of agreed knowledge which constitutes the community: without agreement the group has no basis. This double fact makes it highly desirable that the religious community assert its own existence as a community; it must appear and be experienced as a community. Every religion therefore has celebrations where people come together with one another in order to give expression in some way or other to their shared outlook. This must be seen as the first function of the worship service or other religious ritual: to provide such experience of the community, and reinforcement of the outlook which it exists to maintain. A worship service that does not achieve these will necessarily be ineffective. So long as it does achieve them, what actually takes place at the service may be relatively unimportant. The fact that a sermon is given, for example, may be more significant than what is said in the sermon, provided only that it does not disagree too apparently with the shared outlook of the group, for the fact of a sermon being given by the correct person may be already an acting out of the fundamental viewpoint of the community.

The observations made so far apply to the religious community inasmuch as it is a knowledge-community like any other. However, it is placed in a special position by the fact that it is a community of that knowledge which is the most important. This is that knowledge which supremely makes a difference to me. That is to say, it is in the first instance an interpretation of life, a way of looking at life, not a set of metaphysical or historical facts. The facts make the difference, but it is the difference which is important; the facts are of interest only insofar as they make the difference, and quite different sets of facts can do that, as we have seen. However, as we have also seen, any given interpretation of life is most likely to be expressed in statements which are factitive in character, rather than directly importative, and which function symbolically, or metaphorically.

What then is the knowledge bond which unites the members of a religion: is it that they share the same interpretation of life, or that they share the same symbols? The two do not by any means necessarily coincide. People may have widely differing symbols, yet discover that their fundamental outlook on life is very similar; they may share the same set of symbols, yet discover that they mean very different things by them, and that their outlook on life is thoroughly divergent.

Of the two, the community of life-interpretation is clearly superior to a mere community of symbols. The symbols exist only to establish the community of life-interpretation. But it is the symbol-community which appears. A community of life-interpretation alone is not possible, it must have some form of communication, which will inevitably be symbolic. The religious communities which actually exist are necessarily symbol-communities. There is a dilemma here which creates a constant tension for any religion. The unity of symbolism creates the illusion of a unity of meaning, of vision. But the illusion may be broken by a sudden crisis, or even by simple discussion, theological argument. A reform movement which tries to recall the group to a unity of vision will almost inevitable split it. Unity of meaning can usually only be had at the price of symbolic unity; symbolic unity can generally only be had at the price of unity of meaning. The dilemma is often insoluble. For this reason, as well as for others that will appear subsequently, we must now say that a religion as such does not have an interpretation of life. What it has is the appearance of one, and for many purposes that is enough. It has a symbol-set capable of different interpretations, but its very ambiguity is its advantage. Since people mostly inherit the symbols they use, they are provided with an apparent community, a means of thought and communication, yet one that allows room for their own individuality without the penalty of automatic excommunication—until the individuality becomes too apparent.

This inherent tension in the religious community between symbol and vision is compounded by two further factors: the mixture of continuity and discontinuity in the tradition, and the ambiguous relationship of the individual to the community.

A community enduring through time is a tradition. A tradition is an assertion of continuity; history, however, implies discontinuity. Of course history also implies continuity: we cannot rid ourselves of our past, and even the most novel of events is still the product of previous forces. The discernment of continuity is part of the historian's task; but equally so is the recognition of discontinuity and diversity. History is pluralistic; without discontinuity there would be no history. To speak of history is to speak of change.

Numerous books have been written with the title "The Essence of Christianity." But seen from the outside, from the viewpoint of the historian, there is no such thing as the "essence" of a historical movement. A religious tradition "as such"—"Judaism," "Christianity," "Buddhism"—does not exist anywhere. A ready example of this is "Communism." There are Russian, Chinese, and European varieties, each competing for recognition as a faithful heir of an original vision. Which of these is "real" Communism? The question cannot be answered, it is meaningless. To the outsider it is obvious that there is no such thing: some aspects of Marx's doctrines are preserved in one, other aspects in the others. The Buddhist world is divided between the Theravada and the Mahayana. Which of these is genuine Buddhism? The question can scarcely be asked; they are devoted to quite different aspects of the Buddha's work, the one claiming to follow his doctrine, the other his example. Judaism exists in Orthodox, Conservative, and Reform versions, not to mention the Reconstructionist movement. Is one of these incompatible forms true Judaism, and the others false? The Islamic world is divided into the Sunnite and the Shiite sects, and also includes the Sufi movement. Which of these is "authentic" Islam? For the outsider the question, if it has interest, has no meaning.

There is no such thing as the essence of a tradition existing "out there." What does exist is people. It is they who are the bearers of the tradition, and it exists only in them.

This brings us to the second problem, the ambiguous relationship of the individual to the community. The individual learns the tradition from the community, for that is where it is preserved. Insofar as he is a member of the community he shares the community's vision. It is of the utmost importance for him to have a community of people who share his vision. But he is also a unique individual, with an experience of life which, while it has much in common with that of others, is nevertheless as a totality unique. This unique experience of life is the criterion which decides what makes sense for him and what does not. It is not possible, even if it were desirable, for one person to adopt *in toto* the point of view of another. If his conviction about something is to be genuinely his own, it will often not be identical with someone else's. It can be assimilated and made his own only by interpreting it in the light of his own particular experience. Almost inevitably it is altered in the process. The deeper and more personal my conviction about something is, the more it will be my own and not someone else's. By contrast, the less I am personally involved, the easier it is for me to take over another's view with only limited assimilation. But even the most superficially adopted opinion takes its meaning from the person's experience, and cannot escape being individualized to some degree, if it is to be real at all.

The act of assent which a person gives to the traditions of a religious community is a unique act, insofar as it is the act of a unique person. The tradition itself as a whole comes to each individual in a different form, through different situations, in different languages and therefore different thought-categories, through different groups of people. The act by which he gives assent to some element in the tradition arises out of his own individual personality, out of his own individual experience of life, his reactions to the past, his hopes for the future. He cannot simply appropriate *in toto* a conviction which comes to him from outside himself. Merely to adopt a form of words is cynicism; the sincerity of a person who "repeats the party line" is understandably questioned.

Where then does the tradition exist? It exists on the fluctuating boundary between the individual and the other individuals who make up that community, in the act of encounter between them and in the communication among them. Insofar as they are unique individuals their concrete beliefs will be different. Insofar as they share a vision, they form a community. To the extent that their viewpoints show similarities with one another and with an earlier or original one, we put them together for descriptive purposes, and as it were tie a string around them and label them "Judaism" or "Christianity." Every religious tradition consists of a bundle of viewpoints which merge here and part there. However, disclosures of discontinuity threaten the tradition, since it exists by asserting continuity.

The problem of continuity in a religious tradition can be seen in a number of ways. It can be viewed as the problem of translation: how do you translate a sentence from one language into another and preserve its meaning? It can be seen as the problem of hermeneutics: what criterion do you use to interpret a statement? It can be understood as a problem of substance and form: Pope John XXIII said that the purpose of the Second Vatican Council was to update the form of the Roman Catholic Church's teaching while preserving its substance. The question this raises is whether a distinction can be made between the substance of a belief and its form: if you change the form, how do you avoid changing the substance? What does it mean to speak of the "substance" of a belief?

Some writers have asserted that it is impossible to translate a symbol effectively. All we can do, Paul Ricoeur tells us, is look at it intently, and then it "donates" or "presents its meaning in the opaque transparency of an enigma, and not by translation." In this view the only possible form of hermeneutics or interpretation is by viewing a group of symbols in the perspective of a dominant symbol, and then by participating in the dynamic of the symbols themselves, that is, in the struggle which ensues when one symbol encounters another, since each tends to break the other, while left to itself it tends to atrophy. The only way of comprehending a symbol is by personal involvement with it.

To the extent that symbols are opaque, there is much to be said for this view. It is for this reason that theology is no substitute for religion. Yet the things that we consider symbols are not only opaque. They have a certain area of transparency, and it is this we try to delineate whenever we relate one symbol to another.

For this reason I would prefer to ask the question of continuity, or, what is the same thing, the question of what constitutes fidelity to a religious tradition, not so much in terms of penetrating a symbol, but in terms of metaphor: how do you change a metaphor yet keep its meaning?

Whether a metaphor aptly expresses a meaning cannot be decided by logic. The correspondence of a metaphor to what you want to express by it is not a matter of reason or rationality. It is a matter of *looking* at the metaphor, and looking at what it is intended to say, and *seeing* that it fits. The meaning is then "seen as" the metaphor.

But metaphors of the sort religions are concerned with (i.e., for meanings of the sort religions are concerned with) arise out of particular cultural situations. The cultural situation is thus an *a priori* condition for the meaningfulness of any religious metaphor. It is only in terms of people's experience that a metaphor can have meaning for them, and the quality of their experience is altered with an alteration in the cultural conditions of their life. If a profound modification takes place in the cultural situation even the most significant and powerful metaphors may lose their meaningfulness. We observe this happening at the present time in a particularly striking fashion.

This leads us to conclude that it is not possible to determine in advance what metaphors might be compatible with a certain meaning. The question can only be asked when the concrete historical and cultural situation has changed. That is, it is only in the new situation that it can be seen whether the new metaphor conveys what it is intended to convey, or whether it falsifies the meaning.

The function of a religious community is not exhausted by its being a community of knowledge; it is also a community of purpose, and that of final purpose. That is to say, it is constituted a religious community by the fact that its members not only have the same goal, but that this goal is one which overrides all others. A religious community is distinguished from other kinds of communities in that the purpose which its members have in common is not a partial or intermediate one, but one that embraces human life as a totality. It is from this purpose that the "meaning" of life is derived, whether it is believed to be a purpose inherent to life itself, establishing a meaning intrinsic to life, or whether it is held as a purpose created by the individual and bestowing on life a meaning extrinsic to it. In either case, a religious community is constituted by commonality in that purpose which decides the meaning of life as a whole. The purpose of the religious community is the achievement of the ultimate purpose of human life.

A goal exists as a goal only insofar as it is aimed at. The mere knowledge that life is or can be directed towards a goal suffices of itself to establish a meaning for life only notionally, not really. If life is to possess meaning really or effectively, the goal must be actively striven for. Even where realization of the ideal is considered to be certain, conditions are always attached to the participation of the individual in that ideal state of affairs: there is always something which the individual must do, he is never invited to be purely passive. Failure to act towards that ultimate purpose deprives life of real, or effective, as opposed to notional or theoretical, meaning.

Just as community reinforces conviction so that it becomes knowledge, so it reinforces purpose so that it takes on the social form of authority. A purpose shared by a group becomes authoritative for the individual. The individual is encouraged, and even put under extreme pressure, to show publicly his allegiance to the common cause, and to act publicly towards the realization of the common goal. Social purpose issues in command and obedience, even though these may be well disguised. The acknowledged influence of the peer-age group on the American adolescent is a case in point. A religious community is not only a community of vision, a cognitive community, it is equally a community of activity designed to achieve realization of whatever is considered to be the ideal state of affairs to the extent that that is possible, and participation in that realization if the realization is already certain. The communal activities of religions, such as worship services, communal meditation, etc., must be understood in this light.

This communal action will have a different function, however, depending on the certainty with which realization of the ideal is expected. It happens very rarely, if at all, that the salvation of a particular individual is considered assured while he is still alive. If then realization of the ideal is expected with certainty, it can only take place in a form that is general and public, the participation of the individual in that public salvation remaining dependent on some conditions. By the fact that it is guaranteed to happen therefore, the ideal state of affairs must be communal, and it is to be expected that the participation of the individual in that communal state will be furthered by appropriate communal action now. If the goal is communal and public, it is unlikely to be reached by means that are exclusively private and solitary.

On the other hand, if realization of the ideal is not considered to be certain, but only possible, then there is nothing that will require the goal to be public, and there is not likely to be any than the usual virtue in communal activity designed to achieve it. In this case the religious community supports purpose and hope by communal activity in the way that any community performs those functions for its members, only since its purpose and hope are final rather than partial or intermediate, the communal action needed will have to be appropriate to that finality. In general this can be said to be true of the Chinese and Indian religions. By contrast, in the ethical, Semitic religions and Marxism, where realization of the ideal is expected with certainty, the community and its communal activity have an essential role, integral to the conception of the religion and deriving from the essentially communal nature of ethical concern.

NOTE

The proposition that knowledge is socially determined is derived, not surprisingly, from the sociology of knowledge. The
term "knowledge" is not used here in such a way as to insist on
the truth of what is known. It is to be taken as if in quotation
marks, "knowledge," and means whatever is allowed to count as
knowledge. The question has received much discussion by philosophers whether knowledge is true belief or justified true belief. I prescind from this question here. (I would like to observe
in passing though that the use of the term "belief" in this connection seems confusing. In most of Europe as well as in some
quite large English-speaking circles, "belief" also means "faith"
[*Glaube, foi, fede, fe*] and is often used not for an element of
knowledge, but in contrast to it: if I know something, then by
definition I do not believe it, and vice versa. It might be more
useful to employ some such term as "conviction" in its place,
which is equally neutral as to truth or falsity and has no misleading overtones of trust.)

The observation that knowledge, in this sense, is socially determined has a long history. It was stated clearly by Pascal in his
famous dictum that what is good on one side of the Pyrenees is
bad on the other. Marx made it a premise of his system that "life
is not determined by consciousness, but consciousness by life,"
where by "life" he meant the structure of society. He elaborated
this thesis with a distinction between "substructure," which is
the world of labor and social activity, and "superstructure,"
which is the world of thought and the constructions of thought,
such as law. Wilhelm Dilthey proposed an approach to the study
of history which emphasized that all human thought is bound to
a certain historical situation (*Standortsgebundenheit*), and can
only be understood in light of the function it fulfills there (its
Sitz im Leben).

Against this background Max Scheler initiated the discipline
of the sociology of knowledge (*Wissenssoziologie*), arguing that
the emergence of ideas in history, though not their truth, is
determined by sociohistorical forces (*Realfaktoren*).

With Karl Mannheim the question of the truth of socially
determined knowledge was raised to the level of an explicit
problematic. Marx had assumed that while his opponents'

thought was unreliable because socially determined, he and his colleagues possessed a privileged cognitive position which rendered their own insights true. The two concepts of "ideology" (truth-convictions serving in defense of a social structure) and "false consciousness" (thinking that is alienated from the actual social location of the thinker) applied in Marx's view only to his opposition.

Mannheim saw that they must apply to everyone, including one's own thought. By abolishing the notion of a privileged position, however, an acute problem is raised in that it seems truth is relativized. If everyone's knowledge is socially determined, how can we avoid concluding that truth is relative? Mannheim sought to avoid this by defending "relationism," as against relativism, that is, the influence of social forces on knowledge is not so much to falsify it as to limit its perspective. Knowledge therefore is always only possible from a particular perspective. Another sociologist of knowledge, Werner Stark, has built up a version of the discipline in which it is taken for granted that the effect of social determination is to open access to truth, rather than to distort knowledge.

The figures mentioned so far have understood the term "knowledge" in "sociology of knowledge" to refer primarily to theoretical thought—"ideas" in an intellectual sense, as developed by "men of knowledge." These works have been essays in "the history of ideas," as Stark subtitles his *Sociology of Knowledge*. This conception of the scope of the sociology of knowledge was widened by Alfred Schutz to include the ordinary convictions, beliefs, and thought-categories of ordinary people, in everyday life. This extended scope has been fundamental in the work of Peter Berger and Thomas Luckmann, to whom this author is especially indebted.

Although Berger and Luckmann have both applied sociology of knowledge in this wide sense to religion, they have done so mainly with a view to showing the legitimating function that religion fulfills for society, and exploring the problems that society must face as the result of secularization. That is, they have written naturally enough as sociologists, with their eye primarily on society. The present chapter of this essay is in part an attempt to apply to religions in themselves, as knowledge-communities (e.g., faith-communities), the insights of Berger and Luckmann on the social determination of knowledge.

5. Interest

The deepest wisdom lies in ambiguity.
— Lu Hsin

Our life is dominated by three general forms of interest: curiosity about matters of fact, concern for matters of importance, and enjoyment of the beautiful. Each of these kinds of interest has a way of using language which is peculiarly appropriate to it, and there is also a use of language which combines the three. In each case the function, and therefore the significance, of language is characteristically different. Religious language, as a subtype of one, namely, of concern for matters of importance, is intelligible only in relation to the others, the language of curiosity about matters of fact, and that of enjoyment of the beautiful.

The phenomenon of curiosity merits special attention in this regard. Curiosity is interest in a matter of fact which makes no difference to me. My personal condition is in no way altered by the discovery in Africa of a human skull three million years old, by the red shift in the wave emissions of distant galaxies which indicates an expanding universe, by the existence of a Mayan civilization in central America a thousand years ago. But such matters are capable of being of intense interest. Curiosity is interest in knowledge for the sake of knowledge. It is the play of intelligence. It is a particularly human feature; although animals seem capable of it, their lives are characteristically preoccupied with matters of importance.

All explanations, as explanations, are expressions of curiosity. This is true both of real explanations, which add to our knowledge, and apparent explanations, which do not, but are suprisingly common. If someone says to me: "Isn't it funny the way children resemble their parents in the most unexpected ways!" and I reply, "That's because of their chromosomes," I have not really told him anything except perhaps a new word; the explanation is only apparent; but it is often sufficient. "Explanations" found in textbooks of biology are often more apparent than real. A Chinese surgeon was reported as remarking about the anaesthetic effects of acupuncture, "We know that if something is done, something else happens, but we don't know why it happens." This could stand for many scientific explanations. By contrast, if someone says to me, "Why is that gentleman walking down Fifth Avenue on his hands?" and I reply "Didn't you see the newspaper this morning? He is running for Mayor," I may be considered, by revealing his motives, to have given a real, if limited, explanation of his behavior.

In either case, the function of explanation is to satisfy curiosity. It may of course happen that the facts adduced in explanation of a puzzle make a difference to my personal condition, and it may well be that it was from suspicion of that that I asked for the explanation. In that case however the explanation is no longer functioning simply as an explanation; it has an active effect on my situation, a thing which no explanation, as explanation, can do. No doubt some men are more curious than others. Many have no particular interest in knowledge as such. Aristotle's dictum that all men desire to know may have been uttered in a flush of optimism. The development of sheer curiosity runs parallel with the growth of civilization, and the decline of the one with that of the other. An exclusive insistence on relevance is the mark of an underdeveloped mind.

The systematic exercise of curiosity has given rise to pure science and certain types of philosophy. Mathematics, astronomy, archaeology are obvious instances of enterprises which by their nature have in view the acquisition of knowledge for the sake of knowledge. It is a mistake to underestimate the force which curiosity has exercised in human history. For the European world the beginnings of systematic curiosity can be traced back to the speculations of the Ionic philosophers.

There is a tendency at the present time for the psychological and social sciences to cast doubt on the existence of sheer curiosity; but to the extent that these are carried on as pure sciences, their own existence contradicts any such notion.

Curiosity is interest in matters of no importance, or in matters insofar as they are not of importance, or, alternatively, in matters which acquire importance solely through our interest in them. The activity appropriate to such matters is play. Curiosity is the play of intelligence. Pure science is the play of intelligence with matters of fact. A game is a form of play run according to rules and thereby given a recognizable shape. Most scientists will readily admit that a scientific experiment is a game, a form of play. However, although play is the form of activity by which we deal characteristically with matters of mere fact, that is, of no importance, play is not necessarily restricted to such matters; it is possible to play with matters of importance. Art is the play of the imagination with values of appearance; theology is the play of intelligence (curiosity) with matters of total importance. It stands to reason that any such play with matters of importance will be fraught with a peculiar tension.

Just as this form of interest which is curiosity has its own appropriate activity, namely, play, it also has its own peculiar form of language, namely, factitive language. The function of factitive language is to describe a state of affairs which does not affect the personal condition of the one describing it. The observation, "Alpha Centauri is the nearest star to our solar system," simply utters a "fact."

A fascinating passage on this subject occurs in Conan Doyle's earliest Sherlock Holmes story, *A Study in Scarlet.* Watson has met Holmes in a laboratory, where the latter was conducting an experiment to detect the presence of hemoglobin in minute quantities. It is clear that Holmes has a detailed knowledge of chemistry. But Watson is surprised to discover that Holmes knows next to nothing about literature, politics, and philosophy; he has never heard of Carlyle, for example. Watson's astonishment reaches a climax when he finds that Holmes is ignorant of the Copernican theory and the structure of the solar system. He can scarcely believe that any civilized human being in the nineteenth century could not be aware that the earth travels around the sun.

"You appear to be astonished," says Holmes, smiling at Watson's surprise. "Now that I do know it I shall do my best to forget it."

"To forget it!" exclaims Watson. "But the Solar System!"

"What the deuce is it to me?" Holmes interrupts impatiently. "You may say that we go round the sun. If we went round the moon it would not make a penny worth of difference to me."

Holmes is so completely caught up in his work that he deliberately excludes from his mind any knowledge that does not pertain to the detection of crime. "It is of the highest importance not to have useless facts elbowing out the useful ones." Holmes is preoccupied with matters of importance. The structure of the solar system is a matter of sheer curiosity to him; it is "useless," and it is therefore totally lacking in interest.

The second form of interest, contrasting strongly with curiosity, is concern. Concern is that type of interest which we have in matters which make a difference to our personal condition. These are matters of importance. It may be objected that there are things which we would all agree are matters of importance, yet which do not affect us personally. It is a matter of importance that the human race should continue to exist, yet once I am dead it will not make any difference to me. However, our personal condition can be affected in a great variety of ways. My situation is altered not only by sensations of pleasure and pain, and all those things which are capable of causing them, such as my income, or my relationships with other people. There are things which are more important than pleasure and pain, and one of them is my evaluation of myself, the way I see myself, the attitude I have towards myself. The continuance of the human race is important because I am important, and I am a human being. To deny the importance of the continuance of my race would be to deny my own significance. My personal condition is affected only naively by external states of affairs. There is no state of affairs which is uninterpreted, and the decisive thing is the way I see it, my outlook towards it.

Most of our time is spent with matters of partial importance, things which affect some part of my existence but do not affect my life precisely as a totality: the monthly paycheck and the things it is spent on, an argument with one's wife, the nightly television program, difficulties and successes in business activities, relatives and friends. But in additon to these there are also matters which affect my life as a whole. If it is true, as the Buddha declares, that "the whole of life is suffering," or as the Upanishad states, that "the Imperishable alone is the Real," or as the Bible and Koran say, that there will be a day of judgment for all mankind, these are things which are not merely of partial but of total importance, and are usually considered to be the peculiar province of religion, or parareligions such as Marxism. In any event they are matters which affect my interpretation of life as a whole, although in practice they often occupy only a small part of our attention. All of these matters, however, insofar as they are considered to affect our personal condition, are objects of concern.

Just as there is a form of activity appropriate to matters which are not considered to be of importance, namely, play, so that activity by which we deal with matters of importance as matters of importance is work. The various activities that men engage in to secure their existence are work; business and politics are not instances of play. St. Paul exhorts us, "Work out your salvation in fear and trembling." We would be surprised, though no doubt pleased, if he had instructed us to play at it. The statement is often made that a good marriage has to be worked at. Work is that activity which is the expression of concern: not necessarily with the task worked at, but then with its fruits. The worker on an assembly line may not be particularly interested in the object he is assembling, but he is vitally concerned about the paycheck that it earns.

Just as the form of interest which is curiosity has its own peculiar use of language, which is factitive, so that form of interest which is concern has its own appropriate use of language, which is rhetoric. Rhetoric is the language of concern. This notion is so essential for an understanding of religious language that some elaboration of it is needed.

The attribution of importance or nonimportance is a matter of *attitude*. Rhetoric is language whose primary function is to express or to influence attitudes. A person's attitude to a thing, in turn, is a reflection of the way he sees it in relationship to himself, of his interpretation of it in regard to himself. Rhetoric then can also be described as language whose primary function is not to provide factual information about something, but to alter the way one sees it in relationship to oneself. At the present time the word "rhetoric" has a pejorative connotation: language which is plentiful in quantity but lacking in conceptual content is objectionable. This pejorative connotation, however, is the result of a failure to understand the peculiar function of rhetoric; it is not the job of rhetoric to convey conceptual content, though it may do that incidentally for its own ends.

In 1971 a motion was brought before the United States Senate that U. S. troops be withdrawn from Vietnam by the end of that year. An amendment was introduced to extend the deadline to the middle of 1972. In a television interview the senator who had moved the amendment was asked how he would vote on the original motion if his amendment was rejected. The vote was scheduled to take place the next day, and he had clearly been giving attention to the matter for a long time. His reply to the question, however, was "I don't really know." This is an example of "pure" rhetoric. Taken literally it was obviously nonsense; he knew how he was going to vote. But as political language it made sense. He could not be accused of being in either camp, and his action in moving the amendment could be interpreted either way. Politics cannot be carried on without the use of rhetoric. If we consider the one necessary, we must allow that the other is legitimate.

Examples of the rhetorical use of language abound on all sides. It is by far the commonest function of language. We spend very little of our conversation in factitive observations, conveying information for the sake of information; a good part of the time, however, we talk to people in order to influence their attitudes.

There is a difference between the rhetorical *use* of language and the rhetorical *form* of language. Language has the form or appearance of rhetoric when it conveys no significant conceptual content, but is aimed directly at the listener's attitudes; he does not know more after than before, but his viewpoint has been put under pressure. The form of rhetoric seems peculiarly congenial to the language of advertising; its function is by nature rhetorical. Half an hour of a commercial radio station provides abundant examples daily. "Glurky shampoo gets *all* the dirt out of your hair, gives it *new* body, *true* body, and long lasting *lustre*!"

By contrast, language may have the function of rhetoric while presenting itself in the neutral sheep's clothing of factitive language. Because it is in the delicate business of influencing people's attitudes, rhetoric is often more likely to be effective if it is indirect, if it does not appear to be rhetoric. Frequently the easiest way of altering a person's attitude is by changing his notion of the facts. Whereby any "fact" will do, so long as it achieves the objective. Political language and that used in courts of law seem particularly liable to this device. A set of carefully selected facts, without further embellishment, can be a much stronger argument than a mere appeal. "It was disclosed today that Senator X last year paid no income taxes." Need more be said? Yet it still strikes westerners as quaint that Confucius should have intended to begin his reform of society with "rectification of names."

The gap between the different types of interest which are curiosity and concern throws some light on the persistent lack of communication between such diverse groups as analytic and existentialist philosophers, between minority or underprivileged groups and those with leisure, between liberal intellectuals on the one hand and conservatives and revolutionaries on the other hand. Analytic philosophy is a philosophy of curiosity about matters of fact, whence its attention to logic, science, and language. Existentialist philosophy is a philosophy of concern for matters of importance, the condition of the human race, the authenticity of human existence. Their inability to communicate with one another is not merely the product of disagreement about particular convictions: they simply bore each other; neither is interested in what the other is doing, because they have different *kinds* of interest. The language of minority groups, such as the black community in the United States, is often and naturally rhetoric not only in function but also in form, a language style born of frustration; splendid examples of pure rhetoric can be heard or overheard in almost any conversation between blacks.

The language of majority groups, such as the white community in the United States, while equally rhetorical in function when its position is threatened, is more commonly factitive in appearance; the white community has learned that such language, which appears to be presenting mere facts, performs the function of rhetoric, affecting or upholding people's attitudes, more effectively than language which is obviously rhetorical. The liberal intellectual has become accustomed to using a language which is factitive not only in form but also in function; he is bent on inquiry; the conservative and the revolutionary alike are not interested in inquiry, but in defending or destroying a social system, which is an object of importance. The analytic philosopher, the liberal intellectual can legitimately be said to engage in play, though it may be in a grave and necessary play; the majority group member appears often enough to play, but can usually be counted on to work to defend his interests; the minority group member, the conservative and revolutionary *qua tales* are not playing, but working. The inability of these various groups to communicate with their counterparts is not a lack of agreement, but a lack of interest. They are not *interested* in communication with one another.

The language of religion is rhetoric. The language of religion in exercise, such as the sermon, tends to have the form as well as the function of rhetoric. The language of religion as used reflectively, for example in theology, creedal statements, and the like, tends to be factitive in form, but discloses itself as also rhetorical in function. Occasionally religious language will have the form of poetry, which we have not yet discussed, while still retaining its rhetorical function. It is the function which is decisive.

The theologian and the existentialist philosopher present a special case, as does the artist, whom we have yet to attend to. Although play is the form of activity appropriate to matters of mere fact, that is, insofar as they are not of importance, play is not necessarily restricted to such matters; it is possible, given the perversity of human nature, to play with matters of importance, as noted above. Art is the play of the imagination with values of appearance, matters whose importance consists in their appearance; existentialist philosophy is the play of the intelligence with matters of importance in themselves; theology is the play of intelligence with matters of total importance. But any play with matters of importance is bound to be precarious: it is a sort of *monstrum*. The theologian especially is doomed to a peculiar frustration, because he is caught in a tug of war between the seriousness of the matters of total importance that he is dealing with, on the one hand, and on the other the lack of seriousness of the tool he uses to deal with them, namely, intellectual play. But by some strange twist in the nature of things, play is the instrument of progress as much as work; the scientist by playing with ideas produces the theory of relativity or Keynesian economics, and also a maturing of thought; the poet by playing with words produces a more profound image of human life; and the theologian, by playing intellectually with the religious tradition he had inherited, makes possible a more sophisticated conception of human life.

Some things are matters of importance in themselves. That is, they make a difference to our personal condition by the simple fact that they exist, quite independently of whether we are aware of their existence and effect on us or not, or else they affect us only on condition that we are aware of them, but their value does not consist precisely in their appearance and is not identical with it. These are values in themselves. By contrast, there are things whose value consists solely in their appearance and is identical with their appearance. They make a difference to us exclusively by their "coming to light," their self-disclosure, in that they present themselves to us. This is the characteristic of the aesthetic.

Beauty is not a matter of appearance in contrast to value; the beautiful is itself an exemplification of value. But the value of that which is beautiful is exhausted in its appearance. There is no importance or value concealed behind a resplendent sunset, or a Mozart symphony, of which each is the expression. Their importance consists precisely in being the sunset and the symphony themselves. The term "beauty" is used here to include all the desired effects of a work of art on the aesthetic sensibility of the witness, including that of tragedy and existentialist drama. The question between value and beauty is at least partly a question between reality and appearance. Appearance is not distinct from reality; it is one part of it, the part that appears. Correspondingly there are two types of value; there is the value of that which exists insofar as it appears, and this is the aesthetic value; then there is the value of that which exists in itself, and this is importative value. The whole reality of a work of art is exhausted in its appearance.

The form of interest which consists in response to beauty is aesthetic enjoyment, in contrast to the two other major forms of interest considered above, curiosity about matters of fact, and concern for matters of importance in themselves. Aesthetic enjoyment is interest in that, the importance of which consists in its appearance; it is the satisfaction derived from the perception of value, not insofar as value exists in itself, but insofar as it presents itself to us, and exists precisely in that presentation.

The activity by which we deal with such things is art, which is a special form of play. It is play, because the matters it deals with are not values in themselves, but in appearance. But it is a specially earnest sort of play, because it creates a species of value. A great work of art affects our personal condition, but "at one remove": aesthetic enjoyment is characterized by a detachment absent from the concern we reserve for matters of importance in themselves.

Like curiosity and concern, the form of interest which is aesthetic enjoyment has its own peculiar form of language. There might be a temptation to say it is poetry, but poetry is only one type of it; it includes fairy tales, for instance, which are not precisely poetry. English lacks a comprehensive name for this general kind of language; it is what the German word "Dichtung" conveys.

Aesthetic language, as we may call it, has an immense variety of literary forms. There is a significant difference between those which lose their force once their aesthetic character is discovered, and those that retain it. A poem does not lose its power by the fact that I recognize it as a poem. On the contrary, its particular effect may depend on my recognizing that it is a poem. If I were to take Dante's Inferno as literal history I would dismiss it as nonsense. A fairy tale, however, like Peter Pan, conveys something very different to the child of four years and the adult of forty. Once I recognize that a thing is a fairy tale, I cannot take it with the same seriousness as before, unless perhaps I now take it as an allegory or parable, which is another thing entirely. Myth belongs in this category. Once I realize that a story is a myth, it loses its native force for me. .

Religious language is often spoken of by philosophers as if it constituted a homogeneous type. However, it can appear in the guise of any of the three forms mentioned here: it often has the appearance of being factitive language, as in statements of faith, and in works of theology; it clothes itself in aesthetic garb, especially for ritual purposes. Occasionally it even appears in the language form which is naturally appropriate to it, rhetoric.

The mistake is commonly made of assigning it exclusively to one of these three, usually one of the first two. Either religious language is considered primarily as assertions of fact, and then the question of truth or falsity arises in the same form that applies to facts in general, although here it cannot be settled, as other questions of fact can be, at least in principle, to the satisfaction of the parties interested. Or else religious language is declared to be "symbolic," which of itself does not get us very far. The language of poetry is symbolic; so is the language of myth; yet their function is vastly different. Thomas Aquinas would grant without a moment's hesitation that our most sophisticated philosophical concepts of God, since they are all analogous, are symbolic. Some symbols lose their power once they are recognized, others do not, and the difference is vital. The notion of "symbol" helps us very little. There is no one category into which religious language can be forced in this way. The decisive thing is the function that any given piece of language fulfills.

At the present stage of civilization the three great enterprises of science, religion, and art are clearly distinguished. The three modes of interest each have their own distinct, appropriate language, the factitive, the importative, and *Dichtung*, the aesthetic. However, there is an earlier stage of civilization where these three enterprises are not distinguished clearly from one another. Primitive religion is at the same time primitive science, both pure, insofar as it satisfies curiosity, and applied, insofar as it provides a means for controlling the forces of nature. When a tribe of Australian aborigines do a rain dance in time of drought, there is no particular reason for calling this religion rather than science; it is both equally. Likewise primitive art is not something separate from this primordial unity of religion and science, but an integral part of it. The man who takes part in a rain dance, who carves a statue or paints a picture so that he may have successful hunting, or for the increase of fertility, is doing something which is art, religion, and science all at once. There is a stage in the development of human culture when the things which we call science, religion, and art constitute one undivided enterprise, and the three forms of interest, curiosity, concern, and aesthetic enjoyment, are fused into one.

This primeval unified interest has a language of its own, which is myth. A myth fulfills each of these three functions in an undifferentiated way. It satisfies curiosity by providing explanation; it expresses concern by conveying importance, by telling of a significant difference made to people; and it offers entertainment by its aesthetic form.

Myth is the language of religion before it has been differentiated from science and art. Equally it is the language of science before it has been sundered from religion and art, and of art while it is still one with science and religion. It is the distinguishing feature of mythic language and the mythic mentality that it grasps these elements in an original unity.

The Karadjeri tribe of Australia tells the following story about the origin of the world. In the Dream-time two brothers called Bagadjimbiri came up out of the earth in the form of dingos, and subsequently turned into two human giants. Until the event of their emergence, nothing existed, neither plants nor animals. The two brothers began to name plants and animals, the stars, the moon, etc. and then these things came into existence. Eventually, the pair turned into water snakes and ascended into the sky, where they can still be seen—as what we call the Cloud of Magellan.

The first thing to be noted about this is that it is a *story*. In fact the tribe has a great number of stories about the doings of the two brothers, how they cooked grain before eating it, threw a stick at an animal and killed it, were themselves killed with a spear and brought back to life again. It is not too much to call these camp-fire stories, and even tall stories. They qualify eminently as *Dichtung*.

Equally however these stories provide an explanation of why the world is the way it is: it is this way because the Bagadjimbiri made it so, and this explanation apparently satisfies the curiosity of the tribe.

Equally again, however, the stories have import: if the world and the tribe are to be preserved, men must imitate the actions of the Bagadjimbiri. The tribal rituals are each described as a repetition of things that the two brothers did, and when they are performed the world is created anew. The stories show men the path to salvation.

The myth thus fulfills what to our mind are three distinct functions. But it would be a mistake to differentiate them within the myth. It is one and the same thing which is story, explanation, and the exemplar of salvation.

Religion, science, and art are no longer one enterprise. They have become distinct and often hostile pursuits. This differentiation is part of the growth of human thought; it was necessary. But in the process something irretrievable has been lost. The world of myth is closed to us now, and it is not possible to return to it. Survivals of that world remain, no doubt, but they belong to the past. The very act of recognizing that something is a myth breaks its power over us. Attempts to "save" myth seem misguided therefore, and doomed to failure. No doubt the relationships between the major occupations of the human spirit will change in the future, as they have in the past, and it is very desirable that the splintering of the spirit which has taken place should be overcome in a new unity, but that unity, whenever it comes, will be new, not a revival of the old; it will be a unity which does not ignore the richness gained through differentiation, but includes and transforms it. In the process what we recognize as "religion" may well disappear, just as the activities we know as "science" and "art" may disappear as distinct undertakings. The need for such an integration is felt already. Its achievement will require the development of a mentality as different from our present one as that is from the world of the Dream-time.

NOTE

1 a.) The phenomenon of interest has received surprisingly little systematic attention from philosophers, and even from psychologists.

Søren Kierkegaard described "subjectivity," the cornerstone of his philosophy, as "infinite personal passionate interest" (*Concluding Unscientific Postscript,* I,1) but did not expound the notion of interest further.

Whitehead practically identifies interest with importance. Interest is "the sense of importance" (*Modes of Thought,* 1,4).

Conversely, importance is interest (ibid.). The distinction between interest and importance is one of emphasis, or suggestion. "Interest" suggests "the individuality of details" in the universe, "importance" suggests "the unity of the universe." This close link between interest and importance might seem to rule out sheer curiosity for Whitehead, but probably it does not, and his notion of importance, as of interest, cuts across both the distinction between subject and object. His contrast of importance to matter of fact is more a contrast of life, subjectivity, consciousness, and experience to mere existence.

The notion of interest forms the center, however, of a theory of religion put forward by William A. Christian which deserves more attention than it seems to have received (*Meaning and Truth in Religion*, Princeton University Press, 1964). Christian defines a religious interest as "an interest in something more important than anything else in the universe," or simply as an interest in "that which is most important," a definition with which I wholeheartedly agree, and have attempted to state in my own terms. On this basis he distinguishes religious interest from practical interest, "in the reconstruction of some object of experience," and aesthetic interest, "in enjoyment of an object that makes no other claim." "Most important" he understands as applying not to a person's feelings, but to the object of his interest: it does not tell us about the quality of his response, but about something to which he responds. Christian points out that this provides a functional rather than a substantive definition of religion. Unlike "sacred," which is assigned as an attribute to objects, "importance" assigns a function allowing a variety of attributes to those objects which might fulfill this function.

Conceiving religion in terms of interest gives no particular preference to the Western tradition of theism, as Christian points out. He consistently takes a wide range of types of religion into account in formulating his theory and drawing out its implications. Christian's theory of religion has one further virtue, that it relegates to its proper, namely, a subordinate, place, Rudolph Otto's concept of religion in terms of "the sacred" (*das Heilige*). Christian shows briefly but effectively that the category of the sacred, where it applies, can readily be explained in terms of what is most important, and also that there are forms of religion to which it does not clearly apply.

1 b.) That there exists such a thing as sheer curiosity is force-

fully defended by Aristotle in the opening paragraphs of his *Metaphysics*. Like interest, curiosity receives at present little notice from philosophers or psychologists. With its implication of spontaneity, it presents something of a problem for a thoroughgoing behaviorism in psychology. Nonetheless some attention has been given to it in psychology, and a good collection of material is *Explorations in Exploration*, edited by David Lester (New York, Van Nostrand, 1969), kindly drawn to my attention by a colleague in the field, Richard Burke. The primary argument is whether there really is such a thing as sheer curiosity or not. In the volume mentioned, some mechanisms are proposed to explain exploratory behavior without postulating an innate need to know. The existence of such an innate need is defended in a final essay by A. H. Maslow. A more general, philosophical exploration of curiosity, and especially of its relationship to religion, seems to be quite lacking.

1 c.) "Concern" has been a familiar term in the study of religion since the work of Paul Tillich, in which it is a key idea. Tillich uses the term to explain the idea of faith, which he defines as "ultimate concern," or "the state of being ultimately concerned," and genuine faith as ultimate concern about the truly ultimate, in contrast to idolatry, which is ultimate concern for what is not truly ultimate (*Dynamics of Faith*). Faith as ultimate concern is "reason in ecstasy."

The language of this ultimate concern must never be taken literally. It can express itself appropriately only in symbols. "Faith, if it takes symbols literally, becomes idolatrous." Therefore the language of ultimate concern must contain within itself an element of self-criticism. The one exception to this, the one utterance of ultimate concern that can be taken literally, is the expression "being itself" (*ipsum esse subsistens*) for the truly ultimate.

Although Tillich's work has fallen into disfavor at the present time because of his existentialist cast of thought, his specially Christian and Protestant emphasis, and his often ambiguous or unclear language, nevertheless he has had no successor in the depth of his insight into the heart of religion. The rise to prominence of language analysis in the philosophy of religion has rapidly made it difficult for us to use Tillich's vague, existential language, although a decade ago he spoke intimately to the needs of many. If we continue to leave him on the shelf, however, we are likely to be the poorer for it. He remains the most profound of American religious thinkers.

Tillich's use of "concern" is not unrelated to Heidegger's *Sorge*, and carries a strongly existentialist flavor. I should perhaps point out that the word's use in the present essay does not have existentialist origins and should not be taken in such a sense, but simply as it occurs in ordinary language. (*Sorge*, care or concern, is the key structural element of human existence for Heidegger: it is the very being of man: *das Sein des Daseins, Being and Time*, ch. 6.)

2 a.) The concept of value and its relation to fact has not yet received settled clarification in philosophical value-theory. Curiously, the notion of value itself has been simply assumed, for the most part, rather than investigated by writers on axiology. They have been more interested in questions like the scale of values, or their objectivity, or the act of valuation, the capacities, such as feeling or emotion, by which we apprehend value. Commonly value is assumed to be equivalent to goodness. Thus J. N. Findlay: "We shall employ the term 'value' as a philosophical equivalent of the goodness, the excellence, the desirability or what not" of objects, states, and situations (*Axiological Ethics*, 6). Promise of a more interesting approach is offered at first glance by Ralph Barton Perry, who defined value in terms of interest: "Any object, whatever it be, acquires value when any interest, whatever it be, is taken in it." (*General Theory of Value*, p. 115 ff.) Any object of any interest is a value. Interest, however, he defines in a behaviorist sense as "the affective motor response" of "favor or disfavor," which brings us back to scratch again. It does not seem to have occurred to Perry that one form of interest is sheer curiosity, lacking any implication of approval or disapproval.

2 b.) The relationship between value and fact has been discussed preeminently from the viewpoint of two questions: whether values are objective or subjective; and whether it is possible to derive a value from a fact.

1) The objective character of value has been defended by most continental writers on axiology. For R. H. Lotze, values, though not "real," nonetheless "hold" independently of the activity of a subject. This view has been upheld, at one period or

another in their writings, by Franz Brentano, Alexius Meinong, Max Scheler, and Nicolai Hartmann, and in the United States by W. M. Urban.

The chief opposition to this view has come from the emotivist theory of ethics, according to which the proposition "stealing is wrong" does no more than express an emotion of horror at stealing. Well-known exponents of this view are C. L. Stevenson and A. J. Ayer.

2) On the whole, adherents of the analytic school of philosophy have held that it is not possible to derive a value from a fact, an "ought" from an "is," or prescriptive language from descriptive language. G. E. Moore labelled the contrary view "the naturalistic fallacy" (*Principia Ethica*, 1903). Numerous attempts however have been made with some zeal to commit this alleged fallacy, especially by writers with a scientific or metaphysical interest. One noteworthy effort is that of Stephen C. Pepper (*Sources of Value*, 1958).

3 a.) The enormous quantity of attention now given to myth is a fruit of the Romantic movement of the nineteenth century, with its heightened appreciation both of the nonrational side of human life, and also of the past and of history, in reaction against the preceding insistence of the Enlightenment on rational and stable structure.

Theories of myth have flowered in a luxuriant profusion almost equal to that of the myths themselves. In particular it has been maintained by three diverse schools of thought:

1) That myth is primarily the language of primitive science, or interest in nature, its chief function being explanatory or etiological.

> "Myths are stories which, however marvelous and improbable to us, are nevertheless related in all good faith, because they are intended, or believed by the teller, to explain by means of something concrete and intelligible an abstract idea or such vague and difficult conceptions as Creation, Death, distinctions of race or animal species, the different occupations of men and women; the origins of rites and customs, or striking natural objects or prehistoric monuments; the meaning of the names of persons or places. Such stories are sometimes described as etiological, because their purpose is to explain why something exists or happens." (Burne and Myres, *Notes and Queries on Anthropology*, pp. 210, 211.)

2) That myth is primarily a primitive poetry of nature, the exercise of imagination and fantasy on earth and sky, wind and water, sun and moon. It is to be taken as an expression of artistic interest, the language of aesthetic enjoyment. This view commended itself to the poetic sensibilities of the Romantics, and to the school of "nature-mythology."

3) That myth is primarily religious language, closely linked to cult, pointing out the path of salvation, by a repetition of the primeval events it portrays which allows the participation of the individual. This is in general, as might be expected, the view of religionists, such as Mircea Eliade, but also of anthropologists, such as Bronislaw Malinowski.

Even so trenchant a defender of his own view as Malinowski, however, is prepared to admit to us—once we have conceded his view the primacy—that "it becomes clear that elements both of explanation and of interest in nature must be found in sacred legends," and that myth "has its literary aspect," and "contains germs of the future epic, romance and tragedy." (*Magic, Science, and Religion.*)

3 b.) Paul Tillich coined the phrase "broken myth" to designate "a myth which is understood as a myth, but not removed or replaced." He held that a myth can be recognized as a myth, yet still retain its force. "All mythological elements in the Bible, and doctrine and liturgy should be recognized as mythological, but they should be maintained in their symbolic form and not be replaced by scientific substitutes. For there is no substitute for the use of symbols and myths: they are the language of faith." (*Dynamics of Faith*, ch. 3) Tillich's use of the term "myth" however is very wide: it refers in effect to any combination of symbols of faith. It does not seem that this wide usage is helpful: it is unusual and somewhat confusing. There can be no doubt that "symbolic language" in some sense must be retained—all language is in some sense symbolic, though not necessarily in the special, participational sense that Tillich gives that word. The point of the present essay is that if "myth" is taken in the original sense, as "stories of the gods," essentially narrative in character, it is *not* possible both to break the myth and to keep it, to realize that the story is not true and did not happen, yet still maintain it as the center of one's religious life.

6. Dialectic

> Everything has its "that," everything has its "this." "That" comes out of "this," and "this" depends on "that" —which is to say that "this" and "that" give birth to each other. But where there is birth there must be death. The sage's "this" is also "that," his "that" is also "this." A state in which "this" and "that" no longer find their opposites is called the hinge of the Way.
>
> — Chuang Tzu

Of all the enterprises of men in the modern era the major religions have been most successful in resisting change. The survival of all of them is now threatened. But their general reaction to this threat is a heartfelt conviction that change, except of a minute and preferably unnoticeable kind, is a fate worse than death. In one sense, their instinct is sound. Mere survival is not enough. Institutions have a regrettable tendency to survive long after their decease. It is better to die alive than maintain a deceptive appearance of life when the spirit has departed. Unfortunately even the apparent death-wish of a major religion does not guarantee that it is truly alive.

Progress takes place in a system only to the extent that there is contradiction within it. The lever of change is the negative judgment, that one thing is not another, is different from it, stands in contrast to it. As Hegel put it, if you simply say "all animals" you do not have the science of zoology. That comes only when you differentiate, when you distinguish one animal from another, and say "this is not that." So long as mere sameness prevails, nothing happens.

Every religion begins, so far as its logical structure goes, with a negative judgment, a decision that the way things have been up till now, the prevailing vision of life, will not do, and needs to be changed. The subsequent importative power of a religion is in direct proportion to the force of this initial negative judgment, for it is this that establishes the identity of the religion. Those founders of religions who receive the appellation "prophet" exemplify the negative judgment in religion with exceptional force. One result of this is that prophetic or ethical religions, such as Zoroastrianism, Judaism, Christianity, and Islam, are marked by a special exclusiveness and intolerance. The negative judgment is divisive. If it continues to predominate, as it did in the Reformation churches, sects multiply. Religious energy is intensified in the direction of change.

This dominance of the negative judgment, however, is strictly necessary only at the inauguration of a religion. The heart of the religious enterprise is an affirmative judgment, not a negative one. It unifies the personality. Religion is occupation with that which is considered most important in life. Even without specifying what that thing is, concentration on the most important as such is an assertion of unifying priority. The interpretation of life that a religion provides embraces not one or another partial aspect of life, but life as a totality. Even though at best its view is never more than incomplete, it is an attempt to view the whole. It affirms primacy. The primacy it affirms is not only in the interpretation of life, but also in its direction. It assembles the dispersed forces of life if only for a few moments, and channels them towards overall purpose. Thus it confers on life at least an appearance of comprehensive meaning. On pain of schizophrenia the individual must strive to attain a self-possessed and therefore unified stance towards life. Division against oneself is the common condition of mankind. That does not lessen, but creates, demand for inner unity.

This thrust towards its own kind of unity helps to explain some of religion's more puzzling features. It makes it natural, for example, for people to feel the need of a spiritual leader. A guru or pope is not only a figure of authority; he also presents a focus of formal unity. The same force leads a religion to assert the unity and continuity of its tradition, no matter what the historical facts may suggest.

But above all, the thrust of religion towards unity brings with it a fateful dominance of the affirmative judgment over the negative one. The affirmative judgment is not by itself a force for change, but resists it. Unity is most easily seen as mere sameness. The desire for unity is then a desire for mere stability, for the end of desire. The affirmative judgment does not aim at a harmony of contrasts, much less the harmony of a resolved discord, but at an undialectical tranquility.

The extreme expression of the affirmative judgment in religion is mysticism. The vision of the mystic is a vision of the oneness of all things and of his own oneness with all things: the "One" of Meister Eckhardt, the "substance" of Spinoza, the "that art thou" of the Upanishads. The non-dualist philosophy of Shankara is the supreme translation of the mystic vision from the realm of religion to that of metaphysics. Raymond Blakeney's observation is profoundly true that Eckhardt was one of the world's great "yes-sayers." Every mystic is before all a "yes-sayer." He is not concerned to deny, he seeks the agreement, the unity in things. It has been noted that mystics of different religious traditions have more in common with one another than with their coreligionists. The affirmative judgment is an affirmation of unity.

If the mystic says "yes," the prophet says "no." Prophetic,

ethical religion and mystical religion are born enemies, the mystic trying to enfold the prophet in an embrace that the prophet will have nothing of. The prophet insists on preserving his distinctness, and declares war unilaterally on the desire for mere peace. Fortunately this does not prevent the two roles from being occasionally combined in the same man, a tribute to the flexibility of our race.

A religion dominated by the negative judgment is a religion of battle. A religion governed by the affirmative judgment is a religion of enjoyment, using the word in its widest sense. As a permanent condition neither war nor bliss satisfies. The two require one another. A religion is not satisfactory unless it maintains both in balance: probably an impossible task. European culture has had almost two millenia of a religion of the negative judgment. It can scarcely be blamed for feeling it is time for a change. The effective religion of at least the educated West now wears more of a resemblance to early Buddhism, and in some respects to Confucianism, than it does to Christianity: a preoccupation with the problem of suffering, and the attainment of happiness, with the achievement of harmony in social relationships, and an agnosticism about higher metaphysics.

India and east Asia have devoted about the same length of time to forms of religion saturated with the affirmative judgment. Mankind's ability to absorb this sort of religion should not be underestimated. But here too it is time for a change. Too much bliss begins to cloy. Indian religion urgently needs "the labor of the negative," a good strong dose of the prophetic spirit, to redress the balance. The era of Shiva the Destroyer has arrived. The prospects that Indian religion will actually take this overdue step seem admittedly slight at the moment. China, however, has already taken it. The advent of Marxism to Buddhist China, and of an anonymous Buddhism to the Semitic West, should be seen as a natural process of historical compensation.

Another consideration is relevant here, the stance of a religion towards the values and goals of its society. The commonest situation is that a religion sympathizes with the aims and values of its society and supports them. This is simply the expression of the state of affirmative judgment that a religion moves to once its identity has become distinct and its position secured. It loses the spirit of prophecy, and becomes agreeable. Society, for its part, is happy with this. It has no desire for a religion that will be a sign of contradiction. It is always in danger of collapse and needs support.

The support that religion gives to society should not be undervalued. Whether it is desirable depends on whether the society is desirable. No society is entirely desirable, and few are totally undesirable. The sociologist who remarks that religion functions as a support to society, and thinks by that he has settled the pretensions of religion, perpetrates an obtuse superficiality.

A religion soaked in the mollient torpor of the affirmative is in an unhappy condition, however; inertia is not the prime mark of a living being. A religion that does not at least in some way stand in serious and substantial contradiction to society has either found utopia or is not doing more than half its job.

Ironically, Hinduism, of all religions probably the most in danger of sinking into soggy affirmation, is at present growing in popularity in the United States, though in naive export varieties, because the goal it sets up is the very opposite of the productive and competitive values that have characterized American culture, and because the need for that opposition is now felt. Official Christianity and Judaism have yielded to the languour of their own affirmation in allowing themselves to become identified with the culture. They have even sponsored some of its typical values. But the culture has preserved what they have not, the need for the prophetic protest, the bite of their inaugural negation. Supremely conservative in its home territory, Hinduism represents revolution in a technological society, as any vital form of the Semitic religions would do in India, and as Marxism has done in China. This is an unsurprising dialectic.

Religions perish for all sorts of reasons. Christianity was removed from North Africa by the Muslim conquest, the worship of Mithra from the Roman Empire by imperial edict. But a religion dies first inwardly. It can be destroyed by enemies only when its vision of life no longer arouses enthusiasm among its friends. The Christianity that evaporated before the Arabs in North Africa was no longer that of the martyrs. Simply in order to survive, a religion may eventually have to have recourse to summoning up the audacity of its original insight, which once uttered "no" to a prevailing order. Buddhism in China died long before it was buried. Another vision, effectively negative, now passes judgment in its place.

There is at present on the public scene no satisfactory conception of what constitutes progress for mankind. Both the developed and the developing economies are preoccupied with a technology that sees no value beyond itself, though the human inadequacy of this is now publicly apparent. The religions of mankind are confronted with the historic task of offering a genuine alternative. So far they have failed. They have either ignored the technological society, as in India and China, or they have succumbed to it, as in Europe and North America. A critical yet comprehensive vision of ideal values is lacking. It is questionable whether mankind will remain long resigned to this deficiency.

NOTE

1. The proposition that identity is established by the assertion of difference did not originate with Hegel, but it is in his writings, especially in the *Phenomenology of Mind*, that the conception is most elaborately developed. It may be said to hold on three levels.

On the level of truth in general, negation is not merely an extrinsic aspect or subsequent result of truth, but is a constituent part of it. "Difference" is "an immediate element within truth as such, in the form of the principle of negation" (*Phenomenology*, Preface).

It is on the level of consciousness or subject, however, that negation really enters into its own, as it were. "The portentous power of the negative" is "the energy of thought, of pure ego." "The action of separating the elements is the exercise of the force of understanding, the most astonishing and greatest of all powers, or rather the absolute power." The negative judgment is not a mere dismissal of something as uninteresting or false, to be made once and forgotten about. It is the abiding element of consciousness. "It [the life of mind] is this mighty power, not by being a positive which turns away from the negative, as when we say of anything it is nothing or it is false, and, being then done with it, pass off to something else: on the contrary, mind is this power only by looking the negative in the face, and dwelling with it."

Mind, consciousness, or subject moves towards its own identity by overcoming both mere sameness, but also mere diversity, for identity is not an undifferentiated oneness, but a unity that is truly itself only through the process of unifying the richness of multiplicity: "As subject it is pure and simple negativity, and just on that account a process of splitting up what is simple and undifferentiated, a process . . . of setting factors in opposition, which [process] in turn is the negation of this indifferent diversity and of the opposition of factors it entails." (If zoology is not "all animals," it is also not just the un-unified diversity of animals.) Thus "self-identity working itself out through an active self-directed process . . . is pure negativity."

Negation is not only an intrinsic element within truth as such, and the distinctive feature of mind or subject. It must above all, and for those very reasons, be asserted as an integral element of the Absolute. The Absolute realizes itself only in the process of "mediation," by which it goes out of itself into difference and returns to itself in the *Aufhebung* of this difference. The idea of the Absolute "falls into edification, and even sinks into insipidity, if it lacks the seriousness, the suffering, the patience, and the labor of the negative." The significance of the negative judgment for religion has been understood most profoundly in the present century by Karl Barth.

2. In the Europe of the Enlightenment reflective religion went into hibernation, a decline typified by Goethe's lines:

> "Wer Wissenschaft und Kunst besitzt, der hat auch Religion.
> Wer diese beide nicht besitzt, der habe Religion."

When religious thought began to come to life again in the early years of the nineteenth century, this was through close association with the new culture of the Romantic movement. The Romantic movement was itself at least partly the product of a religious revival movement, Pietism, and Schleiermacher's *Speeches on Religion to Its Cultured Despisers* owed not a little of its impact to a close bond with Romanticism that was natural to it because of their common Pietist origins. The subsequent religious thought of the first half of the nineteenth century, both theological and philosophical, was largely a hymn of praise to the romantic culture of the era. The impact of Darwin and Lyell, and the struggle of religion to digest the method and discoveries of science in the second half of the century, was still part and parcel of this assertion that religion and culture must go hand in hand, and that they both could and eventually would. Both were optimistic about the future. This general view persevered into the twentieth century until World War I in Europe, and later in America. It is commonly known as liberal Christianity.

Already in the midst of nineteenth century liberal, cultural Christianity, however, one urgent voice had been raised against the absorption of religion into culture. Søren Kierkegaard protested that the stance of religion in the face of culture must be not a Both/And, but an Either/Or. There is an "infinite qualitative difference" between time and eternity, between world and God. Kierkegaard's protest was not heard until World War I brought the optimism of the liberals down over their heads. At that point the honeymoon ended. Raising the banner of Christianity Karl Barth declared war on culture.

Christianity, according to Barth, is not the crown of culture, but its contradiction. ". . . doubtful, disturbing. dangerous . . . that which, over against all occurrences in the world, and every deed of man, is incomprehensible, unbearable, unnameable, as the place where not man's health but his illness becomes known, where not the harmony but the discordance of all things resounds, where culture is not so much grounded but rather, together with the partner, unculture, is radically called in question" (Romans, 1922[3], p. 240).

Friedrich Gogarten formulated the opposition between religion and culture equally sharply. Culture and world stand under the judgment of God, and it is the task of religion to proclaim this judgment, not just on one culture or one era, but on culture as such. Nothing is falser than to consider religion "the soul of culture." It is a "sign of disease" when "it becomes one of the most important concerns of those who profess religion, how to establish connection with culture, and how culture can be aided by religion. Unwittingly culture becomes the end, and religion a means to culture." (*Die religiöse Entscheidung*, p. 52)

The most significant general event in religious thought since World War II has been the death of this dialectical theology. The postwar era opened under the sign of Rudolf Bultmann's program to "demythologize" Christianity, i.e., to rid it of those elements that are no longer compatible with contemporary ways of thinking. This was the reemergence of "liberal" religious thought, and it has celebrated a total triumph. Bultmann has defeated Barth, and the central program of Christian theology since, both Protestant and Catholic, has been to accommodate religion to the requirements of culture. The "death of God" movement is merely the most recent culmination of this enterprise, and its now almost unchallenged victory ought to be acknowledged as the end of reflective religion. The position taken in the present chapter is that neither absorption into culture, nor the mere contradiction of it, establishes the identity of religion, but only a truly dialectical relationship between the two.

3. While Roman Catholicism has customarily been distrustful of mystics, Protestant theology has frequently rejected them entirely, especially since Albrecht Ritschl (1822-1889). Ritschl

considered that the two chief features of mystical religion, in his view, namely, flight from the world and ecstatic union with God, were incompatible with Christianity ("unterchristlich"). Ritschl's disciple W. Herrmann continued the assault on mysticism in a widely read book *Der Verkehr des Christen mit Gott*: "The life of Christian faith finds no room within the narrow experiences that it (mysticism) appeals to." A true Christian cannot at the same time be a mystic.

The antithesis between these two kinds of religion was if possible sharpened by the school of dialectical theology in this century. Friedrich Gogarten writes: "We must see clearly that where we want to have both, the immediate mystical union of the soul with God, and the revelation of God in a historical event, and where we think that with this double possession we can escape decision, that there we necessarily remove from both their content, and so the decisive thing: God." (*Die religiöse Entscheidung*, p. 60) Mysticism must be relentlessly rejected: "Mysticism and historical revelation mutually exclude one another so forcibly that a mixture of them destroys both." Emil Brunner lays out in detail and with some acerbity the contradictions between the two forms of religion:

> "The goal that mysticism seeks is the submersion of the individual in the infinite sea of deity, the melting together of I and Thou in the undifferentiated divine unity, the dissolution of the human personality in the impersonal One. By contrast, prophetic-biblical religion always preserves the distance between man and God, the two never mix, sinful man remains forever separated by a gulf from the holy God, the small I subsists in face of the great Thou. The mystical union with God means the end of human personality; but the dualism of biblical religion allows the right and the validity of the human personality to remain." (*Die Mystik und das Wort*, 1924)

This radical distinction between ethical and mystical religion is not by any means universally agreed to. Catholic Christianity and Judaism have never had the same hostility to mysticism, and the right of the Sufi has been acknowledged in Islam since Al Ghazzali. Martin Buber's work with Hassidism is widely known and welcomed. At the present time, in addition to the general movement in favor of mysticism, a number of writers have attempted to achieve a synthesis of mysticism with Christianity, especially in the Catholic tradition. A notable example of this is Dom Aelred Graham, author of *Zen Catholicism*, a title that explains itself, and of *The End of Religion*, more autobiographical, but in the same direction. So far, however, it must be conceded that mystical Christianity resembles other forms of mysticism more than it resembles other forms of Christianity.

7. Recognition

> Nieh Ch'ueh asked Wang Ni, "Do you know what all things agree in calling right?"
>
> "How would I know that?" said Wang Ni.
>
> "Do you know that you don't know it?"
>
> "How would I know that?"
>
> "Then do things know nothing?"
>
> "How would I know that? However, suppose I try saying something. What way do I have of knowing that if I say I know something I don't really not know it? Or what way do I have of knowing that if I say I don't know something I don't really in fact know it? Now let me ask *you* some questions!"
>
> — Chuang Tzu

What would constitute evidence for or against an interpretation of life? On what basis, by what criteria, can we arrive at a vision of human life which we know is correct? Differing interpretations of life may be complementary, but the principal ones on the public scene, the major world religions and Marxism, for example, are incompatible with one another. If we find ourselves faced with the choice between two contradictory interpretations of life, on what grounds can we choose between them reasonably?

On a question which is purely a matter of the relationship between ideas, as in mathematics, considerations of logic or of conventional assumption suffice as evidence. The proposition "the number −1 has a square root" is logically contradictory if the square root of minus one is taken as a simple number, but if it is taken as a complex number or operator the difficulty disappears. The evidence for this common mathematical assertion happens to be a conventional assumption.

On all other matters which are not solely questions of relationships between ideas, evidence must finally consist in some sort of recourse to experience. The general theory of relativity exhibits logical consistency and commends itself by its aesthetic appeal, but its adoption as an accurate statement about the world awaits the proof of experiment. A proposition such as "there is an unlimited number of subatomic particles" can never be directly verified by experiment, since it is only possible to carry out a limited number of experiments; it can be verified only indirectly, e.g., if it should prove a necessary part of a larger theory which can be verified by experiment. In providing grounds for convictions about matters other than logical relationships, there is no alternative to experience.

The evidence for a matter of fact not experienced consists in another, experienced fact. If I am told by a department store that I owe them $1,000 for a camel, and if they then produce receipts with my wife's signature, I am forced to the conclusion: it is a fact that I have bought a camel.

The evidence for an interpretation of facts already experienced, however, that is, for a way of looking at things, may consist not in other, experienced facts, but in *correspondence* between the facts experienced and the interpretation offered. The phenomenon of recognition is a common instance of such an interpretation which takes place after all the available facts are in. I am walking down the street when a lady approaches, looks at me somewhat expectantly, and passes by. I am puzzled by her behavior until it suddenly occurs to me that she was my hostess at a dinner a couple of evenings ago. I have recognized her, though alas too late. What happens in such a process? The mental act of recognition adds nothing to the sense data.

Yet if I see her again she will look different by the very fact that I recognize her. I look at a page filled with dots, and see nothing but dots; then someone says, "Look, there's a face," and then I see a face there. Recognition does not alter my sense perception, yet my experience of the thing is affected perhaps drastically.

Recognition is established as valid by being shared or communicated. I am hiking in the country with a friend who points to a bird on a limb and remarks, "Look, there's a tawny-breasted erk!" To which I may reply, "I very much doubt whether there are tawny-breasted erks in this part of the country." We both see the alleged erk; how can the puzzle of its true identity be solved? If my friend whips a bird book from his pocket and shows an exact replica of the object in front of us thus labelled, he will have validated his recognition by communicating it to me.

Very little of our ordinary conversation is informational, an exchange of mere facts. A good deal of it is directed towards changing the other person's view or interpretation of a thing. He may know the facts as well as we do; we point out to him those that fit in with our interpretation, and leave unmentioned any that do not; and so we convince him, perhaps. An interpretation is verified by displaying or bringing to light certain aspects of an experience, and aspects of the interpretation which correspond to the experience. The result, if the operation is successful, is to make plain the fittingness of one interpretation, and the unfittingness of another, in regard to the same experienced facts. I see a person ahead of me on the sidewalk whom I recognize as an old friend. Before I can reach him he turns into a building and disappears. If I am alone, I have no difficulty deciding who it was; it was obviously Bill Smith. Suppose however that there are two of us, and the other person with me knows Bill Smith equally well, and he denies that it was Bill. The following conversation might ensue: "Don't you remember, Bill had a bulge on the back of his head to the right, just like this man in front of us?" "Yes, but he was always well-dressed; he would never wear a dirty ragged coat and jeans like that." "True enough, but he used to walk with a slouching gait just like that, and a man's dressing habits may change but his walk doesn't."

If religious beliefs functioned as statements about matters of fact, whether metaphysical or historical, the evidence for or against them would be constituted by other facts, which entail or contradict them. But since the function of religious assertions is to convey an interpretation of life, that is, an interpretation of all facts, there cannot be any additional fact which would count as evidence for or against them. The truth or falsity of a religious assertion is given by the appropriateness of the interpretation of life which it expresses, that is, by the fittingness, the correspondence of the interpretation with our human experience as a whole which it purports to interpret. Is there a face among all these dots or not?

The statement of the Mundaka Upanishad, "The Imperishable is the Real," taken as the religious assertion that it is, must be judged true or false according as the overall interpretation of life which it expresses is judged correct or not.

It follows from this that no single religious conviction, such as that of the existence of God, or of a future life, or a judgment, can be validated in isolation. It is always a question of the totality which it expresses, a particular interpretation of life as a whole. This and this alone is the proper object of attempts at validation or invalidation. A vision stands or falls as a whole. That is not to say that it is either entirely right or wrong, that it may not have something to be said for it while suffering from distortion or imbalance; but a vision of life is an intrinsic unity and should be dealt with as such. The attempt, repeated so constantly over the centuries, to confirm or disprove isolated factitive statements as if religious truth were being dealt with is misleading.

Of course such exploration of isolated factitive statements may be undertaken quite properly by any science which has an appropriate method for studying them, such as some forms of philosophy. In that case, however, these matters are not objects of concern, they are not matters of importance, arousing interest because of the difference they make; they are matters of sheer curiosity; the assertion "there exists a supreme being" is then on a level with assertions such as "Cepheid variable stars fluctuate regularly in brightness" or "brachiopods first appeared during the Cambrian epoch."

In order to validate finally an interpretation of life, we should have to see how it corresponds with experience. In order to see how the interpretation corresponds with experience, we should have to have available experience which was not interpreted. However, there is no such thing as uninterpreted experience; not only does it not occur, it is impossible. Interpretation is an integral part of experience. For one thing, it is provided *a priori* by the community. So long as there is community, that is, therefore, from the very first moment of human life, experience is already filled out with interpretation.

It has been pointed out that what counts as knowledge varies from community to community: the kind of thing that counts as knowledge among the cargo cultists of New Guinea differs noticeably from the kind of thing that counts as knowledge in the community of physicists, and the sort of thing that counts as knowledge in a physics laboratory differs remarkably from what counts as knowledge in a divorce court. What counts as knowledge depends on the community, and there is no knowledge apart from community. It is the community which confers upon a private conviction the status of knowledge. The statement that there is no knowledge apart from community does not mean that a man does not have knowledge when he is alone; but whenever he is alone he has emerged from some community, and is dependent upon its knowledge equipment.

The social determination of knowledge leads necessarily to a certain relativism. There is not in practice any such thing as an attainable absolute truth. However, this relativism is not total. There are elements of experience which are common to human beings. We find that all people are capable in principle of communicating with one another; there is no language that is not translatable. If people can make themselves understood to one another, there is some common ground of experience between them, even though it never appears in a pure state without its interpreter's disguise.

Also, physical objects possess cognitively a certain privileged status. There is a low table in this room, and anyone who wishes to come through must walk round it; not only I, who believe in its reality, but a Hindu mystic who declares it an illusion will trip over it. Even if he declares that the bruise on his shinbone is an illusion, it remains a fact that he has an illusory bruise. However, even physical objects are not immune from the vagaries of interpretation; their obstinacy is largely restricted to the senses of sight and touch—the existence of an odor is less easily a matter of agreement than the existence of a solid object, and the deceptiveness of our sense-perception, even of sight, is notorious enough to have provided Descartes with the point of departure for modern philosophy.

The possibility of communication among human beings and the privileged cognitive status of physical objects imply that there are common elements in human experience. Precisely what these elements are, it is not possible to say; that would require that the speaker totally shed his cultural skin. (It might be objected that at least other human beings are a common element in people's experience; yet there are tribes whose term for "human being" extends only to other members of their own tribe.)

Distillation of the common elements of human experience can never occur explicitly because a societal *a priori* is inescapable. But this distillation occurs implicitly in the act of communication itself. Commonality of experience makes communication possible. By that fact, whenever communication is achieved, common elements of experience are asserted. They are the corrective factor in the situation. They are the keel of the boat, tending to bring it back to a state of balance, but hidden below decks. Whenever we speak to one another successfully, there has been implicit a successful appeal to commonality of experience. It functions constantly, but out of sight. Although we never see it, we rely on it, and like some ghost in a haunted house we are forever coming across traces of its presence.

An interpretation of life is brought closer to reality by encountering another interpretation of life. Even if the other interpretation is farther removed from reality than itself, the field of experience appealed to is broadened through the encounter, the corrective factor is enlarged, the keel of the boat becomes heavier.

An interpretation of life is improved by entering into argument with a contrasting one. A genuine argument will be conducted in such a way that each side appeals to experience as it knows it. In this presentation of experience there will be something which stretches the horizons of the other view, but is capable of being absorbed by it, and there will also be material which is indigestible. Deciding what to adopt of the other perspective, and how much of one's own perspective to give up, is like handling the tiller of a sailboat; you must go by the feel of the thing. A person

with a better, more developed, more finely honed sense of
judgment will make wiser decisions. This is not a matter
where wisdom can be abandoned for logic. The personal
equipment of the decider is an integral part of the decision.
Knowledge of factitive truth may be improved by the use of
logic. For the improvement of an interpretation there is no
substitute for that personal faculty of judgment which is
wisdom. The development of such a faculty is the abiding
aim of all education. The notion that logic can replace
wisdom in the attainment of truth about matters of importance is fantasy.

This means, of course, that there is no external criterion
to which a religious belief can be subjected that will publicly establish its correctness beyond any reasonable doubt.
At most it can be established for a particular public, which
accepts that sort of conviction as knowledge. Within a given
group there will be public criteria available for judgment,
within another group the criteria must be expected to be
different. Progress in the attainment of interpretative truth
is thus largely a matter of historical encounter between
communities.

This does not mean there is any guarantee that in each
individual encounter between life-interpretations progress
will result. What it does mean is that diversity of interpretation tends towards self-improvement. The greater the
variety they exhibit, the deeper and more penetrating the
argument between them, the stronger becomes the pull of
reality as it has disclosed itself in the whole experience of
mankind. Over the long haul the process has an inherent
tendency towards self-correction. Absolute truth is never
reached; pure experience is never sifted out; but every time
our interpretation of life is brought up against another that
is foreign to it, the breath of that absolute truth and that
pure experience are felt a little closer. The attainment of

an interpretation of life that is definitively true is an on-going process, self-corrective over the long haul, never completed. We walk forever in the light of dawn, towards a sunrise we shall not see, often stumbling, sometimes going in a circle; but every now and then we may look back and see behind us a landmark that we do not need to pass again.

NOTE

1. In Part II of his *Philosophical Investigations*, Wittgenstein devotes a lengthy section to exploring the phenomenon of visual recognition, or "seeing as. . . ." (He also treats the same subject in the second part of *The Brown Book*, a preliminary, privately dictated manuscript, but the *Philosophical Investigations* represents what he wanted published.) He investigates it because he sees a connection between it and "experiencing the meaning of a word," which is his real interest; but his observations on recognition have some value in their own right, in drawing attention to its epistemological significance.

Using the illustration of the duck-rabbit, a drawing that can be viewed equally as a duck or as a rabbit, he points out that in either case "we interpret it, and *see* it *as we interpret* it." "But how is it possible to see an object according to an interpretation?" In one sense there is a new perception, and yet in another sense the perception is unchanged.

One new element is that a way of organizing the material is noticed which had not been noticed before: "I suddenly see the solution of a picture puzzle. Before, there were branches there; now there is a human shape. My visual impression has changed and now I recognize that it has not only shape and color but also a quite particular 'organization.'

"I meet someone whom I have not seen for years; I see him clearly, but fail to recognize him, I see the old face in the altered one. I believe that I should do a different portrait of him now, if I could paint."

What then, Wittgenstein asks, is recognition? It "seems half visual experience and half thought." "Is it a special sort of see-

ing? Is it a case of both seeing and thinking? or an amalgam of
the two, as I should almost like to say."

Wittgenstein comes to few clear conclusions in this analysis.
One noteworthy one, however, is that "What I perceive in the
dawning of an aspect is not a property of the object, but an
internal relation between it and other objects." Another is that
the concept of "experience" is different, though related, in "seeing" and "seeing as. . . ."

Perhaps the most valuable contribution he makes is the suggestion that the art or game of "seeing as . . ." is something that
does not have rules, but is acquired by that kind of inexpressible
experience in which one gets a feel for doing something. It is a
matter of judgment.

> "Can one learn this knowledge? Yes; some can. Not, however,
> by taking a course in it, but through 'experience.'—Can
> someone else be a man's teacher in this? Certainly. From
> time to time he gives him the right *tip*.—This is what
> 'learning' and 'teaching' are like here.—What one acquires
> here is not a technique; one learns correct judgments. There
> are also rules, but they do not form a system, and only
> experienced people can apply them right."

2. As regards philosophic method both Wittgenstein and Whitehead rely upon intellectual versions of "seeing as. . . ." Whitehead formulated his method explicitly, expecially in *Modes of
Thought*, some passages of which are quoted above (Note to
Introduction). Philosophy in his view does not appeal to "proof";
its method is "sheer disclosure." Whitehead commends his
philosophy to us not by any chain of reasoning, but by presenting it to us in such a way that its coherence is manifest. If we
look at it, we will *see*, he claims, that it is coherent, and that it is
faithful to our experience. He commends his philosophy to us as
a painter commends his painting. Its truth, its validity is a matter
of looking and seeing, not of argument or demonstration.

Wittgenstein similarly indulges little in proof. He suggests a
multitude of viewpoints to us and says in effect, "See it this way
. . . and now this. . . ." (cf. David Pole, *The Later Philosophy of
Wittgenstein*, London, 1958, p. 19, n.) These aspects cumulate
eventually into a comprehensive viewpoint: "Try looking at the
whole matter this way." Like Whitehead his aim is not proof but
disclosure.

3. John Wisdom in his essay *"Gods"* interprets belief and non-belief in divinities as different ways of seeing the world, and points out that we do have methods of trying to settle differences about ways of seeing things. "What is so isn't merely a matter of 'the facts.'" There may be agreement as to "the facts," and yet very different interpretations of them, as in a court of law, when the actions of the defendant are agreed upon, yet it must still be decided whether he was or was not "negligent." This is the point of Wisdoms' now famous parable of the garden, in which he compares theist and atheist to two men who, after examining a garden for a long time and agreeing on all "the facts" it contains, nevertheless disagree as to whether it is being looked after by a gardener.

"The difference as to whether a God exists is more like a difference as to whether there is beauty in a thing." "Suppose two people are looking at a picture or natural scene. One says 'Excellent' or 'Beautiful' or 'Divine'; the other says 'I don't see it.' He means he doesn't see the beauty. And this reminds us of how we felt the theist accused the atheist of blindness and the atheist accused the theist of seeing what isn't there. And yet surely each sees what the other sees." Wisdom treats the matter on the whole primarily as a difference of attitude, or feeling, but "seeing as . . ." is an important element in these attitudes and in his argument.

Wisdom is at pains to point out how we try to settle differences about ways of looking at things, with the implication that we can use the same methods in the question of theism. In law cases of accusations of negligence, for example, "the process or argument is not a chain of demonstrative reasoning. It is a presenting and re-presenting of those features of the case which *severally cooperate* in favour of the conclusion." "The reasons are like the legs of a chair, not the links of a chain." "To settle a dispute as to whether a piece of music is good . . . we listen again, with a picture we look again." "Our two gardeners even when they had reached the stage when neither expected any experimental result which the other did not, might yet have continued the dispute, each presenting and re-presenting the features of the garden favoring his hypothesis." It is Wisdom's implied conviction that if they keep at it long enough, they will be able to reach agreement.

Conclusion

Religion is occupation with that dimension of life which is the most important. The aim of these pages has been simply to develop some implications of this commonplace notion: to examine, in the light of it, the function of religious language and so to ascertain the status of the facts religions claim to have special knowledge of, to set forth the distinctive function of religion in human life and locate it among the other enterprises of mankind, to suggest the sort of thing that counts as evidence for or against a religious position, to point out some significant inner tensions of the religious dialectic, and to indicate how progress may be expected to take place in such matters.

No religion has primarily to do with matters of fact, whether historical or metaphysical. Nor is it to be identified with the self-deluding emotion found in some forms of it. Religion is the exercise of interest in importancy. This is the sort of interest we have in things that make a difference to us. Religion is the exercise of a total or comprehensive interest of this kind. That is, it is interest in things insofar as they make a difference not only to one or another aspect of our life, but to life taken as a totality.

Religion's language is therefore not primarily informative, but rhetorical, directing itself neither to the intellect nor to the emotions, but to attitudes. Because they address themselves to what is the most important, religions confer purpose on life, sometimes by suggesting that life possesses a purpose already, but in any event by holding out an ideal that life is to be directed towards as a totality.

As the expression of a primary mode of interest, religion has kinship with science, the exercise of curiosity, and art, devoted to aesthetic enjoyment. These are also primary modes of interest. There is a stage in the development of cultures when these three have not yet taken shape as distinct undertakings. The language of this undifferentiated interest is myth. For us that stage is past, and attempts to summon up its ghost are vain.

The conservatism of religions is not fortuitous, but expresses their affirmation of primacy in interest and vision. The decision by which a religion commences however is a negative judgment, of disassociation from a prevailing order. An adequate religion would maintain both affirmation and negation in a dialectical balance, a difficult task, not accomplished by any existing major religion.

Evidence for or against a religious position is evidence for or against an attitude expressed in a comprehensive vision. It is not a matter of argument but of recognition.

A religion presents an interpretation of life. The question of evidence is the question as to how adequate the interpretation is, measured against the experience interpreted. Since the two cannot be separated, the question cannot be answered directly. In the course of time, however, as the encounter between diverse interpretations of life widens, the field of experience appealed to is broadened. The first issue for religious thought is, how are we to interpret human life? In these fragments, what kind of face shall we see?